The Ministry of the Standard Bearer

The Symbolic Use of
Flags & Banners in Ministry

by Arletia Mayfield

www.tpspublications.com

The Ministry of the Standard Bearer
Copyright © 2012-2019 Arletia Mayfield

All rights reserved. No part of this publication may be reproduced, stored in a retrieval system or transmitted in any form or by any means electronic, mechanical, photocopying, recording or otherwise. Exodus 20:15

Unless otherwise marked, all scriptures are taken from the King James Version (KJV): King James Version, public domain. Scriptures marked BBE are taken from the Bible in Basic English Version (BBE), public domain. Definitions marked NSECB are taken from the New Strong's Exhaustive Concordance of the Bible: All Greek and Hebrew words are italicized. They are taken from New Strong's Exhaustive Concordance of the Bible, James Strong, 1990 copyright © by Thomas Nelson Publishers.

Book Cover Design by: Franklin Mayfield

eBook ISBN: 978-1-7320773-0-0
Paperback ISBN: 978-1-7320773-1-7

Published and Printed in the United States of America

Dedication

This book is dedicated to my daughter, Shekinah Glory Mayfield. According to rabbinic scripture, your name means the dwelling or settling of the divine presence of God.[1] Shekinah, God literally dwells within you. It is my prayer that you embrace the call to serve, praise, worship and most of all love God all the days of your life. I love you forever baby girl. You are my precious gift from God.

He maketh the barren woman to keep house, and to be a joyful mother of children. Praise ye the LORD.
~ Psalm 113:9 KJV ~

---

[1] Wikipedia.org

And in that day there shall be a root of Jesse, which shall stand for an ensign of the people; to it shall the Gentiles seek: and his rest shall be glorious.

~ Isaiah 11:10 KJV ~

Contents

Preface   7

The Call   11

Introduction   17

Chapter I: Definition of the Standard   21

Chapter II: Historical Basis for the Ministry of the Standard Bearer   27

Chapter III: Jehovah Nissi – The Lord Our Banner   35

Chapter IV: Symbolism of the Standard   41

EXERCISE: Jehovah-Nissi, The Lord our Banner   43

Interpreting Movement by the Spirit of God   46

List of Postures   46

EXERCISE: Moving by the Spirit of the Lord   47

Ministering with Flags, Banners and other Symbolic Worship Tools   49

The Purpose of the Standard Bearer Ministry   50

Specific Ways Flags and Banners can be Used in Ministry   50

CHAPTER V: The Twelve Tribes of Israel   53

Profiles of the Twelve Tribes   57

CHAPTER VI: The Symbolic Meaning of Colors   73

CHAPTER VII: Flag Styles & Worship Tools   79

EXERCISE: Create your own Standard   85

EXERCISE: Write a Summary Statement   89

CHAPTER VIII: Etiquette   91

CHAPTER IX: Pure Ministry   95

Preparation for God's Use   96

Talents and Gifts are not the Anointing   97

Will you surrender your gifts to God?   97

Strange Fire   99

Cain & Abel   100

Ananais & Saphira   104

The Danger of Comparison and Competition   105

Idolatry   106

Yoga   108

Astrology   113

Isis Wings   117

How should we respond to correction?   119

CHAPTER X: In Conclusion   123

List of Illustrations   125

The Prophetic Scribe Publication Mandate   127

About Us   128

Preface

The first time I experienced, what is commonly called, flag ministry was in a church located in Southern Nevada; Las Vegas to be exact. The rented space acquired for Sunday worship service and Wednesday evening Bible study was a banquet hall. The pastor instituted a time of intercession and prayer one hour prior to each service. This time was used to consecrate[2] the space and prepare the atmosphere for a holy people assembling to worship a holy God. We entered the space reverently; even removing our shoes to honor God and acknowledge the foundation of Christ as holy ground. Watchmen guarded each entrance to the building; they served as security. During intercession, the watchman, sometimes, held long poles with large flags attached. Everyone that entered or left the building did so under their watchful eyes. One role of the watchman was to prevent interruptions during intercession. People were not allowed to enter once prayer had begun. This helped to eliminate

distractions and disruptions and motivated people to arrive on time. During intercession, soft music played as the sound of prayer permeated the

---

[2] make or declare (something, typically a church) sacred; dedicate formally to a religious or divine purpose. Source: dictionary.com

atmosphere. Some people sat in chairs reading Bibles and meditating on scripture. Others walked around the room waving flags, praying softly or speaking in their prayer language. Occasionally, the pastor would call an individual to the microphone to pray aloud. I had to get over the fear of being called. This was a training and equipping ministry. He was raising leaders and I knew praying aloud in front of people was part of the training.

I was particularly intrigued by the pastor's ability to interpret the movement of the flags and the colors. Nothing escaped his discerning gaze. Often, he would recite scripture that expressed what God was showing or speaking to him. These observations sometimes set the tone for the sermon or confirmed revelations that the prayer warriors were receiving from God. I knew about interpretation of tongues from the Bible,[3] but this kind of interpretation was unfamiliar to me. My point of reference was the Holy scriptures and the Holy Spirit. God is a discerner of the thoughts and intents of our heart,[4] therefore, is it not within the realm of possibility that God could use a prophet or anyone he chooses to interpret the creative or expressive move of His spirit? In fact, God used some of His prophets to demonstrate His message through symbolism in addition to speaking His words. I'm sure we can agree that some of the things they did and said were very strange and demanded interpretation.

---

[3] 1 Corinthians 14:1-28
[4] Hebrews 4:12

Ezekiel laid on his side for a total of 430 days to symbolize the number of years the people of Israel and Judah had sinned. (390 days for Israel and 40 days for Judah.) [5] Also, he used a sword to cut off his hair and beard, burning a third of it; throwing a third of it into the wind; and hacking the remaining piece, leaving only a few hairs on his garment to demonstrate God's anger toward Israel.[6]

Hosea married a prostitute to symbolize how the people had become adulterers in the eyes of God. Not only did he have to marry her, but he had to endure her adultery to demonstrate how God's mercy endures toward us.[7] He even bought her back when she went astray, symbolizing God's plan to buy us back by sacrificing His one and only son to pay for our sins once and for all.[8]

The pastor of the church in Nevada was a prophet. He shared revelation from God that brought clarity and a deeper understanding of God's Word. It was here that I learned how symbols and metaphors in the Bible lead to deeper understanding of the mysteries of God. They are for those that seek and call out to Him for answers.[9]

---

[5] Ezekiel 1:1-2, Ezekiel 4:5-6
[6] Ezekiel 5
[7] Book of Hosea
[8] John 3:16, Ephesians 1:7
[9] Jeremiah 33:3

The next place the Lord sent me was a church located in the Metropolitan area of Atlanta, Georgia. The ministry of the Standard Bearer was demystified for newcomers and guests with handouts that were included in the church Welcome Packet. It explained the use of flags, tongues, interpretation of tongues and prophecy that

Our grandson, Xavier Mayfield, 3rd generation Standard Bearer

people might experience in the worship service. Everything was done according to scripture in decency and order, and without putting limitations on God. During worship, the children marched, single-file around the perimeter of the sanctuary; each one with a banner over his or her shoulder. Some of the older children carried long poles with banners that waved high above the seated congregation. Women praised God at the altar with flags or danced with colorful tabrets. Some wore dance attire; others wore street clothes. Even a few men waved flags during intercession, praise and worship. The altar was adorned with decorative banners declaring the attributes of God. Occasionally, a shofar was blown. The use of the shofar was also explained in the Welcome Packet. As a scribe, I appreciate when leadership makes a point of writing the vision to make it plain. The Welcome Packet explained what a person might experience in the worship service and the biblical basis for such worship. This was important for visitors from other denominations where certain expressions of worship are not common or allowed.

Little did I realize the Lord was using my talent as a scribe to write a book about the Ministry of the Standard Bearer.

The Call

Everyone called by God to ministry has a testimony about how they were called; this is mine.

As I took note of the unique places the Lord led me and sought understanding about what flag ministry meant to Him; to my surprise, it was more than just dancing with flags. This book documents what God revealed to me concerning this ministry.

I was called to the Ministry of the Standard Bearer through dance. While sitting in church week after week trying to be dignified and proper like everyone else, the desire to worship and praise the Lord with all my heart, mind and strength was like fire shut up in my bones.[10] I was reminded of the prophet, Jeremiah, when he had a word from the Lord that he was commanded and compelled to deliver. The dance burned on the inside of me and grew stronger each week during praise and worship. One day, the Lord instructed me to make worship flags. I had no idea why He wanted me to make flags when all I wanted to do was dance. Nevertheless, I obeyed. Rummaging through some boxes of fabric stored away in the garage yielded two identical pieces of white fabric already cut into the shape of a flag. As I constructed the flags, the Lord spoke to me about every element and directed me to scriptures to meditate on.

---

[10] Jeremiah 20:9

The Pole: I was led to purchase a reed from the garden store for my banner pole rather than a traditional dowel.

A bruised reed shall he not break, and the smoking flax shall he not quench: he shall bring forth judgment unto truth. Isaiah 42:3

And there was given me a reed like unto a rod: and the angel stood, saying, Rise, and measure the temple of God, and the altar, and them that worship therein. Revelation 11:1

And the LORD said unto Moses, "Make thee a fiery serpent and set it upon a pole: and it shall come to pass, that every one that is bitten, when he looketh upon it, shall live." Numbers 21:8

The Fabric: The fabric that God provided for my banners was from the lining of an old wedding dress. It was blemish-free and already cut into the shape that He wanted – like wings, but God said, NOT angel wings as some are called, but EAGLE'S wings.

And to the woman was given two wings of a great eagle, that she might fly into the wilderness, into her place, where she is nourished for a time, and times, and half a time, from the face of the serpent. Revelation 12:14

It was prophetic that this wedding dress was from an abusive marriage that was annulled. Now, the train of the dress was going to be a symbol of freedom that resembled eagle's wings as well as a reminder of how the Lord rescued, protected, and delivered me from the trap the enemy had set for my destruction.

The Color: The color of my banner was white, representing the holiness and purity of God; also, the bride without spot or blemish.

And every man that hath this hope in him purifieth himself, even as he is pure. 1 John 3:3

God is a Spirit: and they that worship him must worship him in spirit and in truth. John 4:24

That he might present it to himself a glorious church, not having spot, or wrinkle, or any such thing; but that it should be holy and without blemish. Ephesians 5:27

The Purpose: During this process, the Lord revealed Himself in wonder and glory and I understood my purpose was to worship Him in spirit and in truth; in purity; in obedience; and with all my heart, declaring that there is none like our God. The flag represented surrender to my Lord, Jesus Christ. In his presence I was completely undone.

The purest form of worship is to be completely surrendered in God's presence.

For who in the heaven can be compared unto the LORD? who among the sons of the mighty can be likened unto the LORD?
Psalm 89:6

Being Commissioned as a Standard Bearer in the Church

God continued to teach me about the Ministry of the Standard Bearer. I diligently recorded everything received from the Lord and presented it to the pastor and co-pastor of the church. I also told them about my burning desire to dance. They said, "Do as the Lord is telling you." So, the next worship service, I moved out into the aisle and began to minister in dance and intercede with flags. Some people looked at me very peculiar. The children pointed and giggled. The ushers received a nod of approval from the pastors, so they just observed. Eventually, the congregation got used to me and I even caught glimpses of revelation on the faces of the spectators, especially the ushers. They were the watchman and gatekeepers.

Children as Standard Bearers

Eventually, the pastors asked me to share the little booklet and teach the children how to intercede and praise with flags. The children were taught the purpose for flags in ministry. They understood their role and what was required of them depending on their Standard Bearer assignment. If they were interceding, they were instructed to memorize a scripture to pray over the congregation as they flagged. Praise dancers used their flags to celebrate our victory through Jesus Christ and as an expression of the freedom we have in Christ. The children were taught to care for the flags as a ministry tool and not treat them like toys. They were also taught to flag carefully and responsibly so they would not hurt anyone, including themselves.

Since that season of new beginnings, the Ministry of the Standard Bearer has evolved as we travel from city to city; state to state and from the U.S.A. to other nations. My primary Standard is white. Ministering purity and holiness is my specific assignment at this time, which explains the content and context of this book.

Introduction

The purpose of the Ministry of the Standard Bearer is to present a biblical foundation for the symbolic use of flags and banners in ministry. It explains how the use of flags and banners can enhance the worship experience in a church or ministry setting, as well as practical and historical applications. Also, it is an instructional guide for ministry leaders that desire to teach the principles of the Ministry of the Standard Bearer from the inside out. For the person that believes they are called to what is commonly known as *flag ministry,* it is a guide to understand how to use flags to honor God.

Is it biblical? Another word for *standard* is *banner*. In scripture, the banner is primarily used as a metaphor for victory or overcoming the adversary through God's power. In this book, you will have an opportunity to examine the standard from a historical, practical and prophetic perspective.

Symbolism and Interpretation

The Ministry of the Standard Bearer is based in symbolism. The Bible is full of symbolism; some of it is explained, but some of it is left to interpretation. Although the interpretation of man can lead to deception, the interpretation of Holy Spirit reveals truth that will not contradict the spirit of God's Word or His intent. We will examine this topic in more detail in the section titled *Symbolism*.

How flags can be used in the church: The use of banners in the church can be **practical** (to give directions, as identifiers, and to decorate the walls of the church building); they can be **symbolic** (to convey ideals like victory, unity and reverence); they can also be used along with music and song as a **tool** in worship and praise.

Acceptable Worship: Since worship flags are often used in worship with music and dance, the most important theme you will notice throughout this entire book is *pure worship*; that is making sure your worship is acceptable to God. When examining the scriptures, you will discover that not everything people offer to God as worship is acceptable to Him. The Bible recounts the things that God has clearly said he does not want (e.g. anything used to worship other gods,[11] offerings given in the wrong spirit,[12] sacrifices given without obedience,[13] or disrespect and irreverence[14]). These are examined in greater detail in the section entitled *Pure Worship*.

Exercises: Some chapters include exercises designed to guide you into a deeper understanding and personal revelation about God, His desires and commands, as well as your specific role in the Ministry of the Standard Bearer. You are encouraged to do the exercises. They will help you prepare your heart for this ministry and discover the various postures you can assume as a Standard Bearer.

Footnotes: Scriptures are located in the footnotes. Verses are provided to help you locate the information referenced and as

---

[11] Exodus 32:1-6, 2 Kings 17:33
[12] Genesis 4:4-5
[13] Matthew 15:8-9, 1 Samuel 15:22
[14] 2 Samuel 6:7

spiritual inspiration to ponder. Footnotes are not comprehensive. There is much more to discover on your own about this topic. Hopefully, this book will inspire you to seek God to discover more about Him, His character and your purpose as a Standard Bearer.

CHAPTER I
Definition of the Standard

In this chapter, we will examine the meaning of the word *standard* **as it is used in the Bible to understand its original intent and purpose. Understanding the origins of the standard will help you understand how to demonstrate these principles in their proper context through the Ministry of the Standard Bearer.**

Since we are laying a biblical foundation for the Ministry of the Standard Bearer, it is important to look up words that have been translated from the Hebrew and Greek language in a Bible dictionary or concordance to understand their original meaning and intent. Sometimes, English dictionaries do not accurately capture the spirit behind the words used in the Bible. The biblical definitions in this chapter demonstrate how some of our modern English definitions fail to capture the essence of God's character and His identity that is embedded in the Hebrew language.[15]

Wisdom is the principal thing; therefore, get wisdom: and with all thy getting get understanding. Proverbs 4:7

Get understanding: Do you remember in Bible study when you discovered that the word *talent* was actually a reference to currency or money? Suddenly, the scriptures were clearer, and you were able to interpret the Word of God correctly. However, even as the biblical definition of the word brings clarity and understanding, when we meditate on scripture rather than merely read the words, Holy Spirit may choose to reveal a deeper truth like the one buried within the Parable of the Talents.[16] For example, when I studied and meditated on the word *talent* (the Greek and English definitions) in the Bible, the Lord showed me how it could represent anything of value that God has given us, including our knowledge, skills and gifts. In truth, using the example of money was an excellent way for Jesus to make his point because money is something that man values. But, what does God value? He values you and everything that He has put in you to bring Him glory. By the way, that also includes your money. The moral of the story is, do not bury (waste) what is of value to God. His original command stands. *Be fruitful and multiply.*[17] And, what about the word *multiply*? It means more than to duplicate repeatedly. It is from the Hebrew *rabah,* which means *to*

---

[15] As detailed in the book: Hebrew Word Pictures - How Does the Hebrew Alphabet Reveal Prophetic Truths
by Frank T. Seekins
[16] Matthew 25:14-30
[17] Genesis 1:28

become great, enlarge, to do much and to make great. Do you see what I mean? Seeking the deeper meaning of God's Word is very illuminating.

Standards, Banners and Flags: Although the words *banner* and *ensign* are often used interchangeably in the Bible, it is important to note that scripture does not refer to the word *flag* in the same context, but instead, it is a reference to marsh, grass or reed [Job 8:11] Strong's #260 *achuw* and 5488 *cuwph*.

The word *flag* is a modern, English definition for what the Bible refers to as a standard, banner or ensign. This is the reason many people refer to the Ministry of the Standard Bearer as *Flag Ministry* or *Banner Ministry*. Most references to physical standards in the Bible refer to the banners that identified the twelve tribes of Israel. As we will discuss in the *Symbolism* chapter, other references to the banner are symbolic. In other words, they do not refer to a physical banner, but are metaphors for what the standard or banner represents from a biblical perspective.

The English definition of *banner* is a piece of cloth attached to a staff and used by nations, states, military, law enforcement, organizations and clubs. Flags and banners may also bear images or mottos. The most common English use of the word *standard* is: A level of quality or what is commonly acceptable.

Below are biblical definitions for the word *standard* along with scriptures that use the word in context.

Standard (5127) NSECB *Heb. nuwc* - To flee, to escape, to put to flight, to depart, to cause to disappear, to hide.
So shall they fear the name of the LORD from the west, and his glory from the rising of the sun. When the enemy shall come in like a flood, the Spirit of the LORD shall lift up a standard against him. Isaiah 59:19

Standard (5251) NSECB *Heb. nec* - A banner, such as was set up on high mountains, especially in the case of invasion, when it showed the people where to assemble. (ensign, pole, banner, sail, sign)
Set up the standard upon the walls of Babylon, make the watch strong, set up the watchmen, prepare the ambushes: for the LORD hath both devised and done that which he spake against the inhabitants of Babylon. Jeremiah 51:12

Standard (1714) NSECB *Heb. Degel* – Banner
And the children of Israel shall pitch their tents, every man by his own camp, and every man by his own standard, throughout their hosts. Numbers 1:52

Standard Bearer (H5263) NSECB *Heb. nacac* – To be sick
And the light of Israel shall be for a fire, and his Holy One for a flame: and it shall burn and devour his thorns and his briers in one day; And shall consume the glory of his forest, and of his fruitful

field, both soul and body: and they shall be as when a standard bearer fainteth. Isaiah 10:17-18

Ensign

Sometimes, the word *ensign* is used interchangeably with *banner* or *standard*, but at other times it was something else like Aaron's Rod that bloomed as a *token* against the Israelites that rebelled against Moses and God[18] or the pole with the brass serpent that God instructed Moses to make to spare the lives of all the snake-bitten Hebrews who looked upon it.[19]

Ensign (226) – *Heb. 'owth* sign, signal
A distinguishing mark, banner, remembrance, miraculous sign, omen, warning 2) token, Ensign, standard, miracle, proof.
And the LORD said unto Moses, Bring Aaron's rod again before the testimony, to be kept for a token against the rebels; and thou shalt quite take away their murmurings from me, that they die not. Numbers 17:10

Ensign (5264) - *Heb. nacac* To be lifted up or displayed. To exalt.
And the LORD their God shall save them in that day as the flock of his people: for they [shall be as] the stones of a crown, lifted up as an ensign upon his land. Zechariah 9:16

Now that we have examined the definitions of the words, *standard, ensign, banner* and *flag,* we can see the subtle nuances between the

---

[18] Numbers 17:10
[19] Numbers 21:4-9

Hebrew, Greek and English language and understand better how they relate to the Ministry of the Standard Bearer.

CHAPTER II
The Historical Basis for the Ministry of the Standard Bearer

This is a brief historical description of the Role of the Flag Bearer (Color Guard) during the U.S. Civil War. It serves as an example of a military tradition that demonstrates some of the basic principles and ideals associated with the purpose for the Ministry of the Standard Bearer.

Can you imagine carrying a heavy flag pole for several hours or days during a battle? Can you imagine being a target without a weapon to defend yourself?

Would you be willing to die for the pride of the tribe, so to speak? That is what was required of the designated band of soldiers known as the Color Guard during the Civil War. They were very brave Flag Bearers that were on the front line of battle, charged with carrying the flag of their nation and/or regiment. It was an honorable post, but plagued with hazards, not the least of which was fatigue.

There were both sentimental and practical aspects of this important duty. The flag was very important to soldiers fighting for a cause. It represented the pride of the nation, their community and everything they stood for. So, it was treated with honor and great respect. In addition, flags were often displayed at rallies, celebrations, ceremonies and even funerals to motivate and inspire the men that followed them, even to death.

The flag identified the troops. It served as a reference point in battle.[20] When the troops were separated and confused, the flag gave them direction and focus. However, because the flag was easy to see in battle from enemy lines, it made the flag bearer the proverbial "bull's eye". Needless to say, the death rate was high for these brave soldiers. Nevertheless, the flag held such value that if a man was injured, killed or just too exhausted to continue, someone else would pick it up to keep it waving. If the flag fell into enemy hands it was considered extremely shameful. This was another reason why the flag was protected with vigilance. Likewise, to capture the flag of the enemy was a victory.

---

[20] McNamara, Robert. "Why Were Flags So Important in the Civil War?" ThoughtCo, Dec. 13, 2018, thoughtco.com/flags-importance-in-the-civil-war-1773716.

This is probably the reason so many patriots that served in wars hold the flag of their nation and regiment in such high regard. It is no wonder that they cannot understand how some of the very people they fought to defend have so little respect for the symbol that compelled them to fight for a nation.

Today, the Color Guard is most popular in ceremonial activities by law enforcement and the military as well as educational and political presentations. High school and college bands incorporate flags, batons, sabers, rifles, and the air blade. Some flag bearers dance to the beat of band music in parades and perform routines prior to, or at half-time, during sporting activities. In this book, this kind of activity is described as pageantry.

How does this relate to the Ministry of the Standard Bearer?

Reverence, loyalty, steadfast determination, unity and the willingness to die for what you believe in is at the very heart of the Ministry of the Standard Bearer. We are soldiers in the army of the Lord and our focus needs to be on the battle at hand[21] - between the darkness of this world and the light of Christ.[22] We have been fitted with armor for this spiritual battle.[23] Yet, as in war, and games of war, most people prefer to be the captain or chief rather than the sacrifice. We thank God that He loved us enough to offer an acceptable sacrifice for our sins[24] - His only son.

---

[21] 2 Timothy 2:4
[22] John 12:46
[23] Ephesians 6:10-18
[24] John 3:16

Whom God has put forward as the sign of his mercy, through faith, by his blood, to make clear his righteousness when, in his pity, God let the sins of earlier times go without punishment... Romans 3:25 BBE

The Ministry of the Standard Bearer is very effective at the front line of worship, praise, intercession, warfare, prophecy and as watchmen. Everything we declare points to the King of Glory. We are true worshipers[25]

Women of Papua New Guinea raising the Standard for Holiness

and we declare that truth with our Standard, which is our identifier. We identify ourselves as children of the Most-High God through Jesus Christ, our Lord and Savior. Holy Spirit is our guide, leading us into all truth. We serve at the pleasure of our King who is the King of Kings.[26] We stand in authority and defense of God's Kingdom on earth for which He has given us dominion[27] and appointed us to be His personal representatives.[28] We gladly lay down our lives for His cause and His friends[29] because first, and

---

[25] John 4:23
[26] Revelation 17:14, 1 Timothy 6:15
[27] Genesis 1:26
[28] 2 Corinthians 5:20
[29] John 15:13

foremost, we are friends of Jesus Christ[30] who desires that none should perish.[31]

The Ministry of the Standard Bearer is more than pageantry, but when we honor our King in presentations and processions, He is lifted according to His promise that when He is lifted up from the earth, He will draw all men to Himself. Therefore, we lift our standards to declare that Jesus Christ was raised from the dead to give us eternal life.

And this is the record, that God hath given to us eternal life, and this life is in his Son. 1 John 5:11

Worship on the front line of battle

In 2 Chronicles, Chapter 20, King Jehoshaphat was threatened by several tribes. So, he **immediately sought the Lord** and **called for all of Judah to fast**. Then, he **prayed publicly to God** in front of all the people of Judah and Jerusalem. He **reminded the Lord** of all His promises to deliver and protect them. While he was calling out to God, the Spirit of the Lord came on a Levite who began to **prophesy**... *"Be not afraid nor dismayed by reason of this great multitude; for the battle is not yours, but God's. Ye shall not need to fight in this battle: set yourselves, stand ye still, and see the salvation of the LORD with you, O Judah and Jerusalem: fear not, nor be dismayed; tomorrow go out against them: for the LORD will be with you."*[32] **The response of the people was to fall before the**

---
[30] John 15:15
[31] 2 Peter 3:9
[32] 2 Chronicles 20:15, 17

Lord and worship God and praise Him with a loud voice. The next day, the people of Judah went up against a multitude, but they had a word from the Lord. Jehoshaphat encouraged the people with these words: *"Believe in the LORD your God, so shall ye be established; believe his prophets, so shall ye prosper." And when he had consulted with the people, he appointed singers unto the LORD, and that should* **praise the beauty of holiness**, *as they went out before the army, and to say,* **"Praise the LORD;** *for his mercy endureth forever."* THIS IS WHAT HAPPENED: ***And when they began to sing and to praise, the LORD*** *set ambushments against the children of Ammon, Moab, and mount Seir, which were come against Judah; and they were smitten. For the children of Ammon and Moab stood up against the inhabitants of mount Seir, utterly to slay and destroy them: and when they had made an end of the inhabitants of Seir, everyone helped to destroy another. And when Judah came toward the watch tower in the wilderness, they looked unto the multitude, and, behold, they were dead bodies fallen to the earth, and none escaped. And when Jehoshaphat and his people came to take away the spoil of them, they found among them in abundance both riches with the dead bodies, and precious jewels, which they stripped off for themselves, more than they could carry away: and they were three days in gathering of the spoil, it was so much.*

I imagine when the enemies came up against Israel and Judah and heard all the celebrating and praising going on, they must have been so confused that they just started slaying one another. Just think about how confused the devil must have been. Likewise, when he comes to intimidate us with fear, he expects us to run, hide or surrender. He doesn't expect us to ignore his threats and celebrate joyfully right in his face. The Standard Bearer can lead people into a victorious attitude by taking a position on the front line of praise and worship to lead people to victory in Christ.

And the fear of God was on all the kingdoms of those countries, when they had heard that the LORD fought against the enemies of Israel. 2 Chronicles 20:29

CHAPTER III

Jehovah Nissi

One of the biblical foundations for the Ministry of the Standard Bearer is found in the historical account and symbolism presented in the Book of Exodus, Chapter 17. Jehovah-Nissi is introduced as the Lord our Banner. From the stone Moses sat upon, to the use of his arms raised like a banner, to the support God gave him through Aaron and Hur and more, the Lord showed himself faithful, strong, true and victorious.

The book of Exodus, Chapter 17, is the only place in the Bible where God is called Jehovah-Nissi. The chapter begins with the children of Israel complaining about the absence of water and

questioning whether God is really with them. Moses called out to the Lord and the Lord instructed him to go to the top of a hill and strike a rock with his rod. Moses obeyed the Lord and the thirst of the people was quenched.

The remainder of the chapter describes the war between Israel and the Amalekites. Beginning in verse 8; *Then came Amalek and fought with Israel in Rephidim. And Moses said unto Joshua, "choose us out men, and go out, fight with Amalek: tomorrow I will stand on the top of the hill with the rod of God in mine hand." So Joshua did as Moses had said to him, and fought with Amalek: and Moses, Aaron, and Hur went up to the top of the hill. And it came to pass, when Moses held up his hand, that Israel prevailed: and when he let down his hand, Amalek prevailed. But Moses' hands were heavy; and they took a stone, and put it under him, and he sat thereon; and Aaron and Hur stayed up his hands, the one on the one side, and the other on the other side; and his hands were steady until the going down of the sun. And Joshua discomfited Amalek and his people with the edge of the sword. And the LORD said unto Moses, "write this for a memorial in a book, and rehearse it in the ears of Joshua: for I will utterly put out the remembrance of Amalek from under heaven." And Moses built an altar and called the name of it Jehovah-nissi: For he said, "Because the LORD hath sworn that the LORD will have war with Amalek from generation to generation."*

God's strength in our weakness
Moses had a plan. He was going to the top of the hill with Aaron and Hur with the rod of God in his hand. The rod was a symbol of

God's miraculous power, protection and provision[33] and it was sure to inspire the troops but, Moses' uplifted hands became heavy and tired. Aaron and Hur got a stone for him to sit on. The stone is significant because it represents the strong foundation of the Lord.[34] Moses could not hold his arms up in his own strength for the duration of the battle. So, when God used Aaron and Hur to come alongside of him to support his tired arms it was symbolic of how the Lord holds us up when we are scared and weak[35]. It is also a demonstration of how we are to support one another. The army was encouraged and victorious whenever they saw Moses' raised arms, but when they were lowered the enemy prevailed. Ironically, raised arms usually mean surrender to an enemy, but when Moses' arms were raised, it meant victory because raised arms in the kingdom of God is a posture of surrender and praise to God. Even in his physical weakness, Moses knew God was strong. On that day, Moses served as a standard for Israel, but it was the Lord that orchestrated the course of the battle. Therefore, when Moses built the altar and named it Jehovah-Nissi (the Lord our Banner), it was not only a memorial, but a public declaration that Almighty God was the banner over Israel that defeated the Amalekites even as he used Moses as a symbol. The Apostle Paul shared a revelation about how God uses man's weakness.

My grace is sufficient for thee: for my strength is made perfect in weakness."[36]

---

[33] Psalm 23:4, Exodus 4:17, 20; 7:15,19,20; 8:1-11;8:16-20, 9:23;10:3-21;10:12,13;10:21,22; 14:21,26,27;17:5,6; Numbers 20:7-10
[34] Isaiah 28:16
[35] Isaiah 41:10
[36] 2 Corinthians 12:9

Power in meekness

Moses is described as very meek, *above all the men which were on the face of the earth.*[37] So, why would God choose the meekest man in the world to lead a revolution? Why not the strongest or the smartest or the wealthiest? Scripture tells us, *But God hath chosen the foolish things of the world to confound the wise; and God hath chosen the weak things of the world to confound the things which are mighty.*[38] Obviously, meek does not mean weak to God. Jesus said, *the meek shall inherit the earth.*[39] He then proceeded to demonstrate the virtue (power) of meekness throughout his earthly ministry, including washing the feet of His disciples.[40] Even in his persecution, death, burial and resurrection, Jesus demonstrated his superior power in meekness.

The Testimony of Jehovah Nissi

Why did the Lord instruct Moses to write the testimony in a book for Joshua and to rehearse it in his ears? After all, Joshua was a witness to the events. He was the preordained successor to Moses. Maybe God did not want him to forget his promise.

*The L*ORD *hath sworn that the L*ORD *will have war with Amalek from generation to generation.* Exodus 17:16

Maybe God didn't want Joshua to forget that the battle was the Lord's.

---

[37] Numbers 12:3
[38] 1 Corinthians 1:27
[39] Matthew 5:5
[40] John 13:1-17

What does this testimony mean for us? We have an enemy too. He uses people, situations and our own mind and emotions against us. He operates in the spiritual realm, but if we walk in the spirit and not in the flesh[41] and remain sober and vigilant,[42] we can avoid the snare of the devil. For we are not ignorant of his devices.[43]

We are instructed to *submit to God; resist the devil and he will flee.*[44] Jesus demonstrated this when He was tempted by satan in the wilderness.[45] He was completely submitted to His father and responded to each temptation by quoting what His father had rehearsed in his ear and had written as a memorial for all His people. Jesus is the fulfillment of the commandments and the law of God. He is the Word of God in the flesh.[46] The Word of God teaches us that when the enemy comes in like a flood to discourage and torment us, the Spirit of the Lord shall lift up a standard against him.[47] We just need to recall (testify) what God has done for us in the past, embrace who He says we are and believe His promises to us about our future. Like Joshua, we must constantly remind ourselves and others that God has a plan for our lives. He is with us every step of the way. Therefore, we rehearse daily by speaking God's promises aloud, so we can hear it in our ears, remember it and allow it to strengthen our faith.

So then faith cometh by hearing, and hearing by the Word of God. Romans 10:17

---

[41] Galatians 5:16-26
[42] 1 Peter 5:8
[43] 2 Corinthians 2:11
[44] James 4:7
[45] Matthew 4:1-11
[46] John 1:14
[47] Isaiah 59:19

CHAPTER IV
Symbolism of the Standard

The Ministry of the Standard Bearer is based in symbolism found in the Word of God. This chapter outlines how the banner (standard) is used as a metaphor in the Bible and how this ministry uses symbolism to convey biblical ideas and principles.

Symbolism is used extensively throughout the Bible. Even the Lord, Jesus Christ, spoke in parables, which were stories that conveyed the spiritual ideas that he taught. The Kingdom of Heaven is a weighty topic. So, the Lord used simple stories about things like vineyards and wineskins to simplify complex ideals in a way that people could understand. Some of the metaphors He used were so shocking that some people even stopped following Him. For example:

Whoso eateth my flesh, and drinketh my blood, hath eternal life; and I will raise him up at the last day. For my flesh is meat indeed, and my blood is drink indeed. He that eateth my flesh, and drinketh my blood, dwelleth in me, and I in him. [48]

The parables of Jesus Christ are allegories (stories that align with spiritual truth). When our Lord spoke in parables, He used symbolism to hide the mysteries of the gospel from some and reveal it to others. In the book of Matthew, chapter 13, verses 10 and 11, Jesus is asked by his disciples *Why do you speak to the people in parables? He answered and said unto them, "because it is given unto you to know the mysteries of the kingdom of heaven, but to them it is not given."* Mysteries were revealed to Jesus' disciples because they followed him; they were intimate with him; they knew him, and they had given up everything to have that special relationship with him. Our Lord is still revealing mysteries to those who seek him. One way we gain a deeper understanding of scripture is to understand the mysteries contained within metaphors and symbolism in the Bible. Revelation from God is prophetic by nature. It is God speaking to us, even prophesying to us, through His word. Some people don't want to go that deep, but the Lord promises to reward those that diligently seek him with all their heart.[49] In fact, the Bible tells us that He is actively searching for those who understand and seek after him.[50]

---

[48] John 6:54-56
[49] Hebrews 11:6, Jeremiah 29:13
[50] Psalm 14:2

Symbolism of the Banner in Scripture

Below, is a list of verses that speak symbolically or prophetically about the banner. The following exercise requires an in-depth study of the scriptures that reflect the spirit of Jehovah Nissi. Study the scriptures, then allow Holy Spirit to reveal the essence of the Ministry of the Standard Bearer to you. If you do this important exercise, you will experience how God speaks to us through His word and you will receive your very own revelation about this ministry.

EXERCISE: Jehovah-Nissi, The Lord our Banner

And Moses built an altar and called its name, [The- LORD-Is-My-Banner] Exodus 17:15

For this exercise, you will need your Bible and your journal.

1) First, pray and ask God to speak directly to you through His Word.

2) Read the scriptures below in context. Read what comes before and after the scripture as Holy Spirit leads.

3) Use your journal to describe the context of the verse. What is happening in the story? What does the banner symbolize in the story?

4) Record what the Spirit of the Lord is saying to you about each scripture. It can be a word, a sentence, poetry or even a sermon. Just record what you receive.

1. *He brought me to the banqueting house, And his **banner** over me was love.* Song of Solomon 2:4 KJV
2. *Thou hast given a **banner** to them that fear thee, that it may be displayed because of the truth. Selah.* Psalm 60:4 KJV

3. *And he will let a **flag** be lifted up as a sign to a far-off nation, whistling to them from the ends of the earth: and they will come quickly and suddenly.* Isaiah 5:26 BBE
4. *And in that day there shall be a root of Jesse, which shall stand for an **ensign** of the people; to it shall the Gentiles seek: and his rest shall be glorious.* Isaiah 11:10 KJV
5. *And he will put up a flag as a sign to the nations, and he will get together those of Israel who had been sent away, and the wandering ones of Judah, from the four ends of the earth.* Isaiah 11:12 BBE

6. *And Moses built an altar and called the name of it Jehovah Nissi: [**The- LORD-Is-My-Banner**]* Exodus 17:15 KJV

7. *Put up a **flag** on a clear mountain-top, make a loud outcry to them, give directions with the hand, so that they may go into the doors of the great ones.* Isaiah 13:2 BBE

8. *All you peoples of the world, and you who are living on the earth, when a **flag** is lifted up on the mountains, give attention; and when the horn is sounded, give ear.* Isaiah 18:3 BBE

9. *A thousand will go in fear before one; even before five you will go in flight: till you are like a pillar by itself on the top of a mountain, and like a **flag** on a hill.* Isaiah 30:17 BBE

10. *And he shall pass over to his strong hold for fear, and his princes shall be afraid of the **ensign**, saith the LORD, whose fire is in Zion, and his furnace in Jerusalem.* Isaiah 31:9 KJV

11. *Go through, go through the gates; prepare ye the way of the people; cast up, cast up the highway; gather out the*

*stones; lift up a **standard** for the people.* Isaiah 62:10 KJV

12. *Let a **flag** be lifted up in the land, let the horn be sounded among the nations, make the nations ready against her; get the kingdoms of Ararat, Minni, and Ashkenaz together against her, make ready a scribe against her; let the horses come up against her like massed locusts.* Jeremiah 51:27 BBE

Interpreting Movement by the Spirit of God

Let them praise his name in the dance: let them sing praises unto him with the timbrel and harp. Psalm 149:3

Below, is a list of biblical definitions for some of the postures you might take while ministering under the influence of Holy Spirit. Read through the list and meditate on the definitions. Then, do the exercise that follows.

LIST OF POSTURES:

PRAISE: Make merry, glory, boast, celebrate, sing, give thanks, confess, glory, triumph, commend

THANKSGIVING: Giving thanks, praise

EXALTATION: Proud, upward, raise up, offer, extol, lofty, take higher, respect, lift up, mount up, excellent, increase

WORSHIP: Bow, bow down, fall down, reverence, stoop, crouch, serve, do, work, labor

INSTRUCTION: Correction, chasten, chastisement, check, discipline, rebuke, nurture

WARNING: Admonish, teach, forewarn, speak before, reveal, call, be warned of God

PROPHETIC: Seer, them that prophecy, hear from God, receive instructions from God

JUDGMENT: Lawful, sentence, condemn, execute, defend, punish, appoint, entreat, order, charge, ruler, overseer, plead, right, cause

INTERCESSION: Fall, meet, reach, entreat, prayer

SUPPLICATION: Show mercy, favor, grace, grief, travail, grievous, be weak, entreat, sorry, thought, pity

PRAYER: Meditate, communicate, thought, entreat, talk, beseech, laid, judge, sorry, travail, supplication, intercession, vow, speaking in other tongues

EXERCISE: Moving by the Spirit of the Lord

1. Meditate on the definitions above as you prepare to pray and worship God through movement.
2. Surrender your body to the Lord through submission and prayer.
3. Select music that creates an atmosphere of praise:
    a. The atmosphere is important, so choose Christian music by a Christian artist.

b. Select instrumental music so you won't be tempted to act out the words of the song (interpretive dance) but rather be moved by the Spirit of God (prophetic dance). The music may be any genre of Christian music, but do not use New Age or secular music for this exercise. You may choose to use audio scripture (words only) for this exercise as well.

c. You may use flags, scarves, streamers, a tambourine or just your body for this exercise.

4. Use a video recording device (camera, computer or phone) to record your dance movements.

5. When you are finished, pray. Ask God to interpret the dance as He sees it.

6. Review your recording (refer to the list of definitions in **Moving in the Spirit of the Lord**) to help you interpret what the Spirit of the Lord is saying through your movements. This is your personal revelation.

7. What scriptures came to your mind as you watched the dance?

8. Write the scriptures and your interpretation of the dance in your journal.

Ministering with flags, banners and other symbolic worship tools

Flag and banner worship should be directed by the Holy Spirit. Colors, movement and even sound can be prophetically interpreted by those in tune with the Spirit of God.

For example, the sound and movement of flags waving in a prayer room can speak to your spirit directly from the Word of God.

*And when they went, I heard **the sound of their wings** like **the sound of many waters**, like **the sound of the Almighty**, **a sound of tumult** like **the sound of an army**.* Ezekiel 1:24 ESV

This is one example of how the sound of flags and their movement, can lead to a revelation about the sound of heaven. True prophetic interpretation happens when the defining authority is the Word of God. God speaks to us through His Word. If a person seeks to interpret the move of God without being familiar with His word, they cannot be certain their interpretation is from God. Reading the Bible and understanding the character of God is essential to accurate prophetic interpretations.

A trained Standard Bearer minister is deliberately surrendered to Christ. They are sensitive to the Spirit of God as they minister with flags. They flow with the Holy Spirit in response to His direction. They worship with reverence and fear of God. They are alert and attentive. They are not puffed up in pride or distracted.

The purpose of the Standard Bearer in ministry is to:

1. **Identify** ourselves as disciples of Christ by demonstrating our love for God and one another;[51]
2. **Be a testimony** of victory in Jesus Christ;[52]
3. **Worship the Lord** in spirit and in truth;[53]
4. **Give direction and guidance** to the body of Christ;[54]
5. **Intercede** for people through prayer and supplication.[55]

Specific ways that flags and banners can be used in ministry include, but is not limited to:

1. Flags, banners or ensigns can be used to **identify a ministry** or organization and may include an image and/or motto.

---

[51] John 13:34
[52] Isaiah 30:17
[53] John 4:24, Revelation 12:11
[54] Psalm 119:105
[55] Ephesians 6:18, James 5:16, Luke 6:28

2. **Intercessors** may use a flag as they pray for people at the altar to symbolize God's covering of love, mercy and grace. *He brought me to the banqueting house, and his banner over me was love.* Song of Solomon 2:4

3. A banner can be used by **watchman** as a symbol of **God's divine protection and strategies.** *Set up the standard upon the walls of Babylon, make the watch strong, set up the watchmen, prepare the ambushes: for the LORD hath both devised and done that which he spake against the inhabitants of Babylon.* Jeremiah 51:12

4. People with the gift of dance may incorporate flags, streamers or timbrels (tambourines) in **their praise and worship.** *Miriam the prophetess, the sister of Aaron, took a timbrel in her hand; and all the women went out after her with timbrels and with dances.* Exodus 15:20

5. Flags can denote **spiritual warfare.** *Set up a banner in the land, Blow the trumpet among the nations! Prepare the nations against her, Call the kingdoms together against her: Ararat, Minni, and Ashkenaz. Appoint a general against her; Cause the horses to come up like the bristling locusts.* Jeremiah 51:27

6. Flags can be used to call for **repentance.** *If my people who are called by my name humble themselves and pray and seek my face and turn from their wicked ways, then I*

will hear from heaven and will forgive their sin and heal their land. 2 Chronicles 7:14

7. A flag can indicate the **presence of God and his readiness to heal and perform miracles.** *For an angel went down at a certain season into the pool, and troubled the water: whosoever then first after the troubling of the water stepped in was made whole of whatsoever disease he had... Jesus saith unto him, Rise, take up thy bed, and walk. And immediately the man was made whole, and took up his bed, and walked.* John 5:4,8-9

CHAPTER V
The Twelve Tribes of Israel

Another biblical foundation for the Ministry of the Standard Bearer is found in the original Standard Bearers - the Twelve Tribes of Israel. Their standards identified the tribe of each son of the patriarch, Jacob. The standards also served to organize the people and give direction as they traveled. This chapter offers a profile of each of the Twelve Tribes of Israel with a description of each of their standards.

And the children of Israel shall pitch their tents, every man by his own camp, and every man by his own standard, throughout their hosts. Numbers 1:52

Jacob's Story (in a nutshell): The Twelve Tribes of Israel were established through the bloodline of the twelve sons of Jacob. Jacob was the son of Isaac and the grandson of Abraham. Jacob conned his brother, Esau, out of his birthright, then ran away to live with his uncle, Laban. While there, Jacob fell in love with Laban's daughter,

Rachel, and wanted to marry her. Laban agreed, but tricked Jacob into marrying his eldest daughter, Leah, instead. Jacob eventually gained Rachel's hand in marriage after serving her father for a total of twenty years. When he finally left Laban's house with his wives and children and everything he had earned, his uncle was hot on his trail, accusing him of theft and betrayal. They eventually negotiated a pact before the Lord and Jacob and his family were free from Laban. However, before reuniting with his estranged brother, Esau, Jacob wrestled all night with an angel for a blessing. In the end, he received his blessing, a limp from a hip displacement (compliments of the angel of the Lord) and a new name, "Israel" because the angel said, *For you have struggled with God and with men and have prevailed.*[56]

These are the names of the twelve sons of Jacob and their mothers:

Reuben, Simeon, Levi, Judah, Issachar and Zebulun were born of **Leah**;
Joseph and Benjamin were born of **Rachel**;
Gad and Asher were born of Leah's maid, **Zilpah**;
Dan and Naphtali were born of Rachel's maid, **Bilhah**.

These twelve sons and their descendants were the twelve tribes of Israel with two exceptions:

- Joseph's two sons, Manasseh and Ephraim, were joined together into Israel as one tribe of Joseph.

---

[56] Genesis 27-31

- Levi had no territory of his own, because the Lord, Himself, became their inheritance.[57] Levi's descendants served as priests and were dispersed among the other tribes; that is why even though Levi was a son of Jacob, he is excluded from the list of the twelve tribes.

Standards of the Twelve Tribes of Israel (Shivtei Yisrael)

There is much controversy about the exact symbols, colors and designs of the standards of the twelve tribes of Israel. And, since there has been enough research done on this topic to determine that no one really knows for sure the exact details of each standard, we will not debate the matter in this book. Instead, our focus is on the character of each tribe. Upon close examination of each tribe's standard you can see how the prophetic blessings bestowed upon them by their birth father, Jacob, and their spiritual father, Moses, marked their character and

---

[57] Joshua 13:14, 33

correlated with their achievements. The legacy of each son was literally etched into the fabric and emblems that represented their tribal standard.

Breastplate of the High Priest/Breastplate of Judgment *(Hoshen)*

The breastplate of the High Priest was also known as the Breastplate of Judgment (because the Urim and Thummim were placed in a pocket that was sewn on the inside). These stones were sometimes used to determine God's will in matters that needed to be judged. The breastplate was attached to the Ephod and contained twelve stones with the name of each son engraved upon it. There were also two onyx stones on each shoulder with the names of the twelve tribes. However, once again, there are differing opinions about which stone represented each tribe, the order of the stones and exactly what names and order were engraved on the onyx stones. The fact is, no one really knows for sure. Much of the information available on this topic is from the Midrash (a genre of early rabbinical literature that provides commentaries and interpretations of the Torah). The purpose of this book is not to debate theories, but to form a basic profile of each tribe as it relates to their identity and their standard.

Profiles of the Twelve Tribes of Israel

The following is a basic profile of each tribe. As you examine their legacy, pay close attention to the symbolism in the prophetic words spoken into their lives. Later, you will be asked to examine your own legacy and receive instruction about how to create your own standard.

REUBEN: First born son of Jacob
MOTHER: Leah
NAME MEANS: Behold a Son
STONE: Odem (carnelian, ruby)
STANDARD: Red with an image of mandrakes (a plant)

JACOB'S BLESSING: *Reuben, thou art my firstborn, my might, and the beginning of my strength, the excellency of dignity, and the excellency of power: Unstable as water, thou shalt not excel; because thou wentest up to thy father's bed; then defiledst thou it: he went up to my couch.* Genesis 49:3-4

MOSES' BLESSING: *Let Reuben live, and not die; and let not his men be few.* Genesis 33:6

OTHER FACTS ABOUT REUBEN:
- Reuben was the brother that convinced his other brothers not to kill Joseph, effectively saving his life.[58]
- Reuben dishonored his father by sleeping with his concubine, Bilhah.[59]

CHARACTERISTICS: *Strength, excellence, compassion, dignity, power, unstable, hindered, disrespectful, dishonored.*

SIMEON: Second born son of Jacob
MOTHER: Leah.
NAME MEANS: Hearing
STONE: Pitdah (Topaz)
STANDARD: Green with an image of the city of Shechem

JACOBS BLESSING: *Simeon and Levi are brethren; instruments of cruelty are in their habitations. O my soul, come not thou into their secret; unto their assembly, mine honour, be not thou united: for in their anger they slew a man, and in their selfwill they digged down a wall. Cursed be their anger, for it was fierce; and their wrath, for it was cruel: I will divide them in Jacob, and scatter them in Israel.* Genesis 49:5-7

MOSES' BLESSING: There is no specific blessing from Moses for the tribe of Simeon.

---

[58]Genesis 37:21
[59] Genesis 35:22

OTHER FACTS ABOUT SIMEON:
- Simeon and Levi slaughtered the men of Shechem (son of Hamor the Hivite – the ruler of the area) because he raped their sister.[60]
- Joseph detained Simeon in Egypt as a ransom for his younger brother Benjamin.[61]

CHARACTERISTICS: *cruel, outcast, dishonorable, anger, violence, vengeful, fierce, cursed.*

LEVI: Third born son of Jacob
MOTHER: Leah
NAME MEANS: Joined
STONE: Bareket (emerald)
STANDARD: White, red and black striped with an image of the twelve-stone breastplate (Ephod).

JACOB'S BLESSING: Levi shared his father's blessing with Simeon.[62] *Simeon and Levi are brethren; instruments of cruelty are in their habitations.*[63] *O my soul, come not thou into their secret; unto their assembly, mine honour, be not thou united: for in their anger they slew a man, and in their selfwill they digged down a wall. Cursed be their anger, for it was fierce; and their wrath, for it was*

---

[60] Genesis 34:2
[61] Genesis 42:19-24
[62] Genesis 49:5-7
[63] Genesis 34:2

cruel: I will divide them in Jacob and scatter them in Israel.
Genesis 49:5-7

MOSES' BLESSING: *... they shall teach Jacob thy judgments, and Israel thy law: they shall put incense before thee, and whole burnt sacrifice upon thine altar. Bless, LORD, his substance, and accept the work of his hands; smite through the loins of them that rise against him, and of them that hate him, that they rise not again.*
Deuteronomy 33:10-11

OTHER FACTS ABOUT LEVI:
- Levi had no territory of his own. The tribe was dispersed among the other tribes.[64] The priesthood was drawn from this tribe.[65] They were charged with the responsibility of caring for the Tabernacle of Meetings.[66]
- The tribe of Levi was rewarded for taking a stand for the Lord, even at the expense of the lives of their sons and brothers.[67]

CHARACTERISTICS: *cruel, outcast, dishonorable, anger, violence, vengeful, fierce, loyal, trustworthy, priests.*

---

[64] Numbers 1:49
[65] Numbers 1:50
[66] Numbers 1:53
[67] Exodus 32: 26-29

JUDAH: Fourth born son of Jacob
MOTHER: Leah.
NAME MEANS: Let God be Praised
STONE: Nofech (carbuncle/red) *some believe this stone was greenish, blue*
STANDARD: Sky blue or red with an image of a lion

JACOB'S BLESSING: *Judah, thou art he whom thy brethren shall praise: thy hand shall be in the neck of thine enemies; thy father's children shall bow down before thee. Judah is a lion's whelp: from the prey, my son, thou art gone up: he stooped down, he couched as a lion, and as an old lion; who shall rouse him up? The sceptre shall not depart from Judah, nor a lawgiver from between his feet, until Shiloh come; and unto him shall the gathering of the people be. Binding his foal unto the vine, and his ass's colt unto the choice vine; he washed his garments in wine, and his clothes in the blood of grapes: His eyes shall be red with wine, and his teeth white with milk.* Genesis 49:8-12

MOSES' BLESSING: *Hear, LORD, the voice of Judah, and bring him unto his people: let his hands be sufficient for him; and be thou a help to him from his enemies.* Deuteronomy 33:7

OTHER FACTS ABOUT JUDAH:

- Judah became the most powerful and important tribe of all the Israelite tribes.[68]

---

[68] 1 Chronicles 5:2

- Jesus Christ was a descendant of the tribe of Judah.[69]
- Other notable people from the tribe of Judah include: King David (son of Jesse), King Solomon (son of King David), Mary (mother of Jesus, the Christ), Joseph (earthly father of Jesus, the Christ) and Caleb (son of Jephunneh the Kenizzite. Spy during the Israelites' journey to the Promised Land).[70]

CHARACTERISTICS: *praiseworthy, victorious, respected, ruler, successful, wealthy, prosperous*

DAN: Fifth born son of Jacob
MOTHER: Bilhah (Rachel's handmaiden)
NAME MEANS: Judge
STONE: Leshem (jacinth)
STANDARD: Sapphire blue with an image of a serpent

JACOB'S BLESSING: *Dan shall judge his people, as one of the tribes of Israel. Dan shall be a serpent by the way, an adder in the path, that biteth the horse heels, so that his rider shall fall backward. I have waited for thy salvation, O LORD.* Genesis 49:16-18

---

[69] Matthew 1:1-6, Luke 3:31-34
[70] 1 Chronicles 2

MOSES' BLESSING: *And of Dan he said, Dan is a lion's whelp: he shall leap from Bashan.* Genesis 33:22

OTHER FACTS ABOUT DAN:
- The tribe of Dan fell into idolatry.[71]
- Samson was a son of the tribe of Dan.[72]
- Dan was the one of the largest tribes of Israel (second to Judah).[73]

CHARACTERISTICS: *judge, idolatrous, greedy, self-willed*

NAPHTALI: Sixth born son of Jacob
MOTHER: Bilhah (Rachel's handmaiden)
NAME MEANS: my wrestling
STONE: Achlamah (amethyst/light purple)
STANDARD: purple or lavender with an image of a gazelle, deer or running stag

JACOB'S BLESSING: *Naphtali is a hind let loose: he giveth goodly words.* Genesis 49:21

MOSES' BLESSING: *O Naphtali, satisfied with favour, and full with the blessing of the LORD: possess thou the west and the south.* Deuteronomy 33:23

---

[71] Joshua 18:30-31
[72] Judges 13:2-24
[73] Numbers 1:39

OTHER FACTS ABOUT NAPHTALI:
- Lived in the high places of the field.[74]
- Fought alongside David.[75]
- They were the first on the West of the Jordan to be taken captive.[76]
- Jesus Christ spent much of his public life in lands within the boundaries of Naphtali.[77]

CHARACTERISTICS: *Swift, blessed, fertile, encouraging*

GAD: Seventh born son of Jacob
MOTHER: by Zilpah (handmaiden of Leah)
NAME MEANS: Good Fortune
STONE: Shevo (agate)
STANDARD: Grey with an image of a troop or camp

JACOB'S BLESSING: *Gad, a troop shall overcome him: but he shall overcome at the last.* Genesis 49:19

MOSES' BLESSING: *Blessed be he that enlargeth Gad: he dwelleth as a lion, and teareth the arm with the crown of the head. And he provided the first part for himself, because there, in a portion of the lawgiver, was he seated; and he came with the heads of the*

---

[74] Judges 5:18
[75] 1 Chronicles 12:34
[76] 2 King 15:29
[77] Matthew 4:15

people, he executed the justice of the LORD, *and his judgments with Israel.* Deuteronomy 33:20-21

OTHER FACTS ABOUT GAD:
- Gad fought with Reuben and the half-tribe of Manasseh for the land God promised them.[78]
- Gad continued to fight for the inheritance of the other tribes as well.[79]
- Built an altar called Witness (as a witness between us that the Lord is God)[80]

***CHARACTERISTICS:** Obedient, valiant, warriors, courageous, faithful*

ASHER: Eighth born son of Jacob
MOTHER: Zilpah (Leah's handmaiden)
NAME MEANS: Happy
STONE: Tarshish (chrysolite)
STANDARD: Opal with an image of an olive tree

JACOB'S BLESSING: *Out of Asher his bread shall be fat, and he shall yield royal dainties.* Genesis 49:20

MOSES' BLESSING: *Let Asher be blessed with children; let him be acceptable to his brethren and let him dip his foot in oil. Thy*

---

[78] Joshua 12:6, 13:8-13
[79] Numbers 32:18
[80] Joshua 22:34

shoes shall be iron and brass; and as thy days, so shall thy strength be. Deuteronomy 33:24-25

OTHER FACTS ABOUT ASHER:
- Asher was one of the six tribes that stood on Mount Ebal to pronounce curses.[81]
- Asher possessed fertile land along the Mediterranean coast.[82]
- Asher failed to fight Jabin, a Canaanite King, during the time of Deborah and Barak.[83]
- Asher responded to Gideons call for help against the Mideonites, Amalekits and enemies from the East.[84]

CHARACTERISTICS: *Wealthy, humble, obedient, prosperous*

ISSACHAR: Ninth born son of Jacob
MOTHER: Leah
NAME MEANS: Man of Hire
STONE: Sapir (sapphire)
STANDARD: Black with an image of the Sun and Moon or a laden donkey

JACOB'S BLESSING: *Issachar is a strong ass couching down between two burdens: And he saw that rest was good, and the land*

---

[81] Deuteronomy 27:15-26
[82] Joshua 19:24-31
[83] Judges 5:17
[84] Judges 6:35

that it was pleasant; and bowed his shoulder to bear and became a servant unto tribute. Genesis 49:14-15

MOSES' BLESSING: *And of Zebulun he said, Rejoice, Zebulun, in thy going out; and, Issachar, in thy tents. They shall call the people unto the mountain; there they shall offer sacrifices of righteousness: for they shall suck of the abundance of the seas, and of treasures hid in the sand.* Deuteronomy 33:18-19

OTHER FACTS ABOUT ISSACHAR:
- During wilderness journey they marched on the east of the Tabernacle with Judah and Zebulun.[85]
- One of the six tribes that stood on Gerizim during the blessing and cursing ceremony.[86]

CHARACTERISTICS: *wisdom, knowledge, rest, burden bearer, strong*

ZEBULUN: Tenth born son of Jacob
MOTHER: Leah
NAME MEANS: Dwelling
STONE: Yahalom (beryl/diamond)
STANDARD: Silver with an image of a ship

---

[85] Numbers 2:5
[86] Deuteronomy 27:12

JACOB'S BLESSING: *Zebulun shall dwell at the haven of the sea; and he shall be for an haven of ships; and his border shall be unto Zidon.* Genesis 49:13

MOSES' BLESSING: *And of Zebulun he said, Rejoice, Zebulun, in thy going out; and, Issachar, in thy tents. They shall call the people unto the mountain; there they shall offer sacrifices of righteousness: for they shall suck of the abundance of the seas, and of treasures hid in the sand.* Deuteronomy 33:18-19

OTHER FACTS ABOUT ZEBULUN:
- The Prophet/Judge Deborah praised the Tribe of Zebulun when they participated in the battles led by her and Barak.[87]
- During the time of Moses, the tribe of Zebulun was divided into three clans named after his sons (Seredites, Elonites and Jahleelites).[88]
- Upon entering the Promised Land, Zebulun did not drive out the inhabitants of Kitron or Nahalol. Instead, they forced them to work, which was not what God told them to do.[89]
- Zebulon was among the troops that joined David in Hebron to transfer the Kingdom of Saul to David.[90]

---

[87] Judges 4:6, 5:18

[88] Numbers 26:26

[89] Judges 1:30, Numbers 33:52

[90] 1 Chronicles, 12:23, 33

CHARACTERISTICS: *wealth, courage, valiant, victorious, honored, faithful, loyal*

The tribe of Joseph was split into Manasseh and Ephraim (the names of his two sons). Because the tribe of Joseph was split, it was called the House of Joseph.

JOSEPH: Eleventh born son of Jacob
MOTHER: Rachel
NAME MEANS: May Yahweh Add
STONE: Shoham (onyx)
STANDARD: Black with an image of Egypt or Two oxen (one domesticated/one wild)

JACOB'S BLESSING: *Joseph is a fruitful bough, even a fruitful bough by a well; whose branches run over the wall: The archers have sorely grieved him, and shot at him, and hated him: But his bow abode in strength, and the arms of his hands were made strong by the hands of the mighty God of Jacob; (from thence is the shepherd, the stone of Israel:) Even by the God of thy father, who shall help thee; and by the Almighty, who shall bless thee with blessings of heaven above, blessings of the deep that lieth under, blessings of the breasts, and of the womb: The blessings of thy father have prevailed above the blessings of my progenitors unto the utmost bound of the everlasting hills: they shall be on the head of Joseph, and on the crown of the head of him that was separate from his brethren.* Genesis 49:22-26

MOSES' BLESSING: *And of Joseph he said, Blessed of the LORD be his land, for the precious things of heaven, for the dew, and for the deep that coucheth beneath, And for the precious fruits brought forth by the sun, and for the precious things put forth by the moon, And for the chief things of the ancient mountains, and for the precious things of the lasting hills, And for the precious things of the earth and fulness thereof, and for the good will of him that dwelt in the bush: let the blessing come upon the head of Joseph, and upon the top of the head of him that was separated from his brethren. His glory is like the firstling of his bullock, and his horns are like the horns of unicorns: with them he shall push the people together to the ends of the earth: and they are the ten thousands of Ephraim, and they are the thousands of Manasseh.* Deuteronomy 33:13-17

OTHER FACTS ABOUT JOSEPH:
- After being banished from Potiphar's house and sent to jail, Joseph was put in charge of the prisoners in jail.[91]
- Jacob blessed Ephraim over Manasseh, a privilege usually reserved for the eldest son.[92]
- Manasseh and Ephraim received equal inheritance to Jacobs other sons even though they were two half-tribes.[93]

CHARACTERISTICS: *trustworthy, wise, responsible, dominant, steadfast, compassionate, favored*

---

[91] Genesis 39:22
[92] Genesis 48:18-21
[93] Genesis 48:5

BENJAMIN: Twelfth born son of Jacob (youngest)
MOTHER: Rachel
NAME MEANS: Son of the Right Hand
STONE: Yashpeh (jasper)
STANDARD: Multi-colored with image of a wolf

JACOB'S BLESSING: *Benjamin shall raven as a wolf: in the morning he shall devour the prey, and at night he shall divide the spoil.* Genesis 49:27

MOSES' BLESSING: *And of Benjamin he said, The beloved of the Lord shall dwell in safety by him; and the Lord shall cover him all the day long, and he shall dwell between his shoulders.* Deuteronomy 33:12

OTHER FACTS ABOUT BENJAMIN:
- After the death of Ish-Bosheth, Benjamin joined the Tribe (Kingdom) of Judah and eventually lost their identity after Babylonian captivity.[94]
- Most of the tribe of Benjamin were wiped out after the Battle of Gibeah.[95]
- Notable Benjamites include: King Saul, Jonathan (son of King Saul), Mordecai (cousin of Esther who adopted her) and the Apostle Paul.

---

[94] 2 Kings 24-25, Jeremiah 25, Ezra, Nehamiah
[95] Judges 20

CHARACTERISTICS: *predator, beloved, protected, men of valor, pugnacious*

CHAPTER VI
The Symbolic Meaning of Colors

Most of the colors listed in this chapter have symbolic meaning that is revealed in scripture from the Bible. However, there is room for prophetic interpretation.

When we minister with flags, we want to speak the language of the kingdom, even though we are not using words. Therefore, the best way to use colors in the Ministry of the Standard Bearer is to use them according to the language and pattern of the Holy scriptures.

Some colors listed are not specifically mentioned in the Bible. Colors with no scripture notations are included because of their popularity in the Standard Bearer ministry. The Standard Bearer may receive a prophetic interpretation for the use of a color or a combination of colors, but sometimes, the interpretation will come from an observer or intercessor. Nevertheless, there will usually be a biblical reference associated with any interpretation.

For International Standard Bearers:

Keep in mind that colors have different meaning in cultures around the world. Some of these perceptions are based in superstition, some in patriotism and some in tradition. Also, the common use of flags may be different. They may only be used in pageantry, theatrical productions or military exhibitions. If you are ministering with flags in foreign countries or to a specific people group of a different culture, it's wise to make sure the colors you choose are not offensive or compromise the message of your faith.

Here are a few examples:

- In Indian culture, red represents purity, fertility, wealth, power and beauty.
- In South American culture, red is associated with mourning.
- In Thai tradition, red is the color for Sunday. Each day of the week is assigned a specific color that is linked to a god. It is also associated with Surya, a solar god who was born on a Sunday.
- In Chinese culture, red is worn on New Year's Day. [96]
- In Haiti, red, blue and black flags represent voodoo gods.

Research colors. Pray and seek God about what colors to use whenever you minister with flags. Since flags are used for other purposes and some people may not be familiar with them being used as an instrument of worship, it's a good idea to educate people about

---

[96] SOURCE: Smartertravel.com

the Ministry of the Standard Bearer when you can. It will help them understand your purpose. In the list below, colors with * are not listed in the Bible, but may be popular or have prophetic relevance.

After studying the scriptures associated with colors, allow Holy Spirit to guide you in the selection of the colors you choose when ministering with flags. [97]

AMBER: God's Glory (Ezekiel 1:4, 1-27, 8:2), **Christ as Glory of God** (Ezekiel 1:4, 1:27-28; 8-2) KJV

BLACK: sin (Job 6:15-16), **disease** (Job 30:30), **famine** (Lamentations 4:8, 5:10, Revelation 6:5-6) **death** (Jude 1:12-13), **sorrow** (Jeremiah 8:21), **judgment** (Jeremiah 14:2; Leviticus 13:37, Job 3:5)

BLUE: heavenly (Exodus 24:10, Ezekiel 1:26, 10:1), **priestly garment** (Exodus 28:31, Esther 8:15), **chastisement** (Proverbs 20:30); **Also used to represent revelation, peace, eternity, truth, royalty, grace, mercy.**

BRASS: Jesus' feet (Revelation 1:15)

CRIMSON: sin (Isaiah 1:18), **blood/life** (Genesis 9:4-5, Deuteronomy 12:23), **sacrifice** (Exodus 12:13; 23:18), **remission of sin** (Hebrews 9:22, 1 John 1:7, Revelation 1:5), **covenant** (Exodus 24:8, Matthew 26:28, Romans 5:9, Hebrews 9:12; 13:12), **war** (1 Kings 2:5, 1 Chronicles 22:8)

---

[97] SOURCE: Ridingthebeast.com

GOLD: God's divine nature, glory, majesty & kingdom (Exodus 28:36, Psalm 11:4; 21:3; 199:72)

GRAY: old age (Genesis 42:38, Deuteronomy 32:25, 1 Samuel 12:2, Job 15:10, Psalm 71:18), **beauty of old age** (Proverbs 20:29), **weakness** (Hosea 7:9), **ash – worthless** (Genesis 18:27, Job 30:19), **destruction** (Exodus 9:10, Ezekiel 28:18, Malachi 4:3, 2 Peter 2:6), **purification** (Numbers 19:17), **sorrow** (2 Samuel 13:19), **mourning** (Esther 4:3, Jeremiah 6:26), **repentance** (Job 42:6, Matthew 11:21), **scattered** (Psalm 147:16)

GREEN: rest (Psalm 23:2), **life** (Isaiah 15:6, Psalm 23:2, Ezekiel 17:24, Luke 23:31), **growth** (Ezekiel 17:24), **fruitful** (Jeremiah 11:16, 17:8, Hosea 14:8, Luke 23:31), **fresh/undefiled** (Song of Solomon 1:16, Luke 23:31), **maturity** (Job 15:31-32), **frailty** (Psalm 37:2); **Also used to represent new beginnings, harvest, abundance and prosperity.**

*IRRIDESCENT: Sometimes used to represent Holy Spirit, transparency and heavenly.

*PINK: love, intimacy, innocence

PURPLE: royalty (Judges 8:26), **riches** (Revelation 18:16, Luke 16:19), **corruption of riches** (Revelation 17:4); **Also used to represent authority, power, dominion, God's Holy temple and God's Kingdom.**

RAINBOW: God's promises (Genesis 9:12-13), **Radiance of God** (Ezekiel 1:28, Revelation 4:3; 10:1)

RED: war (2 Kings 3:22, Nahum 2:3), **vengeance** (Isaiah 63:2), **temptation** (Proverbs 23:31), **winepress – God's wrath** (Revelation 14:19-20); **Also used to represent the blood of Jesus, Fire, Love & Passion.**

SCARLET: cleansing/purification (Leviticus 14:4;52, Numbers 19:6, Hebrews 9:19), **sin** (Isaiah 1:18), **the raiment of a valiant man** (Nahum 2:3), **riches** (Revelation 18:12:16), **sign – passover** (Joshua 2:18-21, Genesis 38:28)

SILVER: truth (Psalm 12:6); Also used to represent redemption, Word of God, God's wisdom & refining process.

VERMILION: unrighteousness (Jeremiah 22:13-14); **lust** (Ezekiel 23:14)

WHITE: purity, refinement, unblemished, righteousness, heavenly (Psalm 51:7, Ecclesiastes 9:8, Daniel 7:9; 11:35; 12:10, Matthew 17:2, Mark 9:3, Luke 9:29, John 20:12, Acts 1:10, Revelation 3:4-5; 18; 4:4; 6:11;7:9; 13-14), **victory** (Revelation 6:2: 19:11;14), **angelic** (Mark 16:5); **Also used to represent cleansing and holiness.**

CHAPTER VII
Flag Styles & Worship Tools

There are a variety of flag styles to choose from and they are often chosen for their beauty and style. However, the flag(s) chosen by a Standard Bearer should have a specific purpose (choosing the best tool for the job). Invite Holy Spirit to direct your flag selection. What does God want accomplished? Remember that as a Standard Bearer your priority is ministry. Your goal is not to impress people with your talent or the beauty of your flag or garment. Ultimately, you want to see the power of God move people by His spirit to salvation, repentance, deliverance and godly transformation. To be genuinely effective, a Standard Bearer must be free of sinful behavior, attitudes and thoughts and totally surrendered to God.

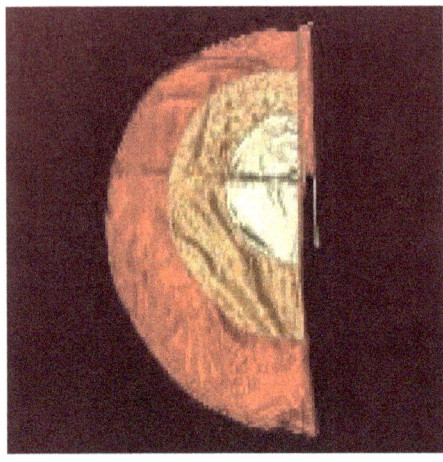

Half-circle worship flags (also called Angel Wings) are very popular and are typically used in praise, worship and dance.

Small worship flags are appropriate for waving and for children. They are especially useful inside buildings.

Worship flags can be used for waving, dancing or declaring. They can be a variety of sizes.

Swing Flags are rod-less flags. Weights are sewn into the fabric to balance flags while twirling. These flags can be stored in a small bag or purse when not in use.

Large Pole Flags are often used to identify, proclaim, guard and establish territory. They are also used in processions at the front or end of the line.

A Billow is a large, long rectangular flag that can be used by one or more people to create a wave. One or more billows may be used together with people on each end to

create a wave-like movement that can symbolize the movement of Holy Spirit, waves of the ocean, wind, pulling down (blessings, strongholds), lifting or raising (petitions, praises) and more. Sometimes, people walk under the billows to symbolize God's banner of love that is over them.[98] Billows are sometimes used in theatrical productions and group settings.

Large Hanging Banners are often used to decorate the interior walls of a sanctuary or they may be suspended from the ceiling. They may also be displayed on stands, on conference tables or carried on a pole in a procession. Some banners display scripture, serve as ministry identifiers or declare a specific message. They also make wonderful backdrops for recitals and theatrical presentations.

A Scarf can represent a veil to denote purity or modesty. It can be flown overhead like wings. It can also cover someone being ministered to for healing or deliverance.[99]

---

[98] Song of Songs 2:4
[99] Acts 19:12

In Acts 19:12 handkerchiefs (which is a type of scarf) were brought to the Apostle Paul (for him to touch), and when they were given to the sick, diseases and evil spirits departed from them.

Worship Streamers are long and graceful. They can be made from ribbon or fabric and are fun and easy to use. Streamers are often used in dance, performances and in celebrations.

Tabrets and Timbrels are like a tambourine. They are used in praise, worship[100] and spiritual warfare[101]

---

[100] Exodus 15:20, 2 Samuel 6:5, Psalm 149:3
[101] Isaiah 30:32, Ezekiel 28:13

Worship Garments are worn specifically for ministry. They are typically loose fitting and cover most of the body. Dance worship garments may be as basic as palazzo pants and long, flared skirts to more elaborate costumes with embellishments.

A note about Isis Wings:

One garment that has received a makeover in an attempt to make it acceptable for Christian worship is a garment called, *Isis Wings*. Christian bookstores renamed and repackaged them as *Angel Wings* and worship dancers now use them in ministry. Isis Wings are worn by belly dancers and give honor to the goddess, Isis. We will examine this and other idolatrous practices that have crept into the church in the final chapter of this book entitled *Pure Worship*.

There are various poles used in flag and banner ministry. Below, are a few of the most popular styles:

    a) the wooden dowel is a rounded stick. It is used with large and small worship flags as well as streamers.

    b) Extension rods extend in length to enable flags to fly higher.

c) Spinning rods twirl freely on the pole. They are made using a solid rod inside of a hollow rod.

d) Quill or flexi-rods are flexible rods that flex and bend with movement.

Your identity in Christ

Now that you have examined the biblical, practical and prophetic aspects of the Ministry of the Standard Bearer; the profiles of the original Standard Bearers (The Twelve Tribes of Israel); flag styles and colors, it's time to create your own standard that reflects your identity in Jesus Christ.

EXERCISE: Create your own Standard

Begin by answering the questions below in your journal. After reviewing your notes, write a summary describing what the symbolism of your standard declares about you. If you desire, draw or create an actual standard (banner or flag) and/or ensign (image or design) for yourself.

Things to consider when creating your standard:

a. What size will your standard be? Consider where it will be used.

b. What kind of pole will it have? Consider how it will be used.

c. What is the shape of your standard? What does the shape communicate?

d. What color is your standard? Why did you choose the color?
e. What symbol or image best represents your identity in Christ? Draw an emblem for yourself.
f. What words have been spoken over your life that have shaped your identity? If the words spoken over you do not reflect what God says about you, reject them and create a new narrative based on what God says about you in His word.
g. What scripture best reflects who you are in Christ? Find one or more foundational scriptures that describe your purpose, mission or identity.

What's in a Name?

In the Bible and many cultures, names are important. As we observed in the names given to the sons of Israel, names can make an indelible impression on a person's personality. Use the internet to investigate the meaning of your name. SEARCH: *Biblical meaning of names.* If you cannot find your first name, try your middle name or your last name or the root of your name. Ask your parent(s) how your name was chosen? What is the root of your surname (last name)? If your name does not line up with who God says you are, write down scriptures that affirm your identity in Christ or ask God to give you a new name. You don't have to change your name legally, but God may give you the name of your ministry. If the words spoken over you as a child or adult do not reflect the way God sees you, refer to the Bible to find scriptures that reflect who God says you are.

1 Chronicles 4:10 describes how a man named Jabez was given a name that labeled him. His name meant *pain*. His mother gave him that name because of the pain she experienced in childbirth. In his prayer to God, Jabez asked the Lord to bless him and enlarge his territory and to keep him from evil so that he would not cause pain. The Bible tells us that God honored his request.

Below is an example of how I came to understand my identity in Christ. It is included to demonstrate how I created a summary statement based on what the Lord revealed to me about my identity.

The Creation and Interpretation of the Standard of The Prophetic Scribe

The root of my first name *Arlette* means *like an eagle*. My middle name means "cascade or waterfall." Somewhere, I read that it also means *Holy*. The Lord gave me the name, *The Prophetic Scribe* through the mouth of a prophet. She said that's what the Lord called me. I had never heard of the term, but the Lord helped me understand my purpose as one who has been called to write from the heart of God prophetically, administratively,

This unedited photo became the cover for my first book.

instructionally and creatively. My emblem is a writing instrument. The Lord exemplified this on the cover of my first book. The untouched photo was my finger writing in the sand with a beam of sunlight right next to mine (the finger of God). The beam was discovered after the film was developed. The graphic designer wanted to correct it. She saw it as a flaw, but I understood that the Lord was affirming me, and I knew this photo was the cover of my book.

My standard is white - symbolizing holiness and purity. This is the color the Lord chose for me when He instructed me to make my first set of flags out of fabric from an old wedding dress that was cut into the shape of what He described as *Eagle's Wings*. Holy Spirit put Revelation 12:11 in my heart and revealed my assignment to *unlock* the people of God to tell the stories that set people free. That is why my writing is often testimonial. I write to encourage people to dig deep inside of themselves to unlock the treasure within. Later, the Lord trained me as a Standard Bearer. Do you see the prophetic call on my life as a Prophetic Scribe and a Standard Bearer? The interpretation is below.

I am prophetic. I am a scribe that writes from the heart of God. My hand is, literally, led by Him. I am a bride of Christ ministering God's holiness and cleansing grace with white flags. When I minister, a cascade of living water bursts forth to quench the thirst of

hungry souls. I have Eagle's Wings to soar because the Son has made me free. I am a testimony of truth through transparency. I use my gifts and talents to unlock the people of God to tell the stories that help set others free.

~Arletia Mayfield, The Prophetic Scribe~

EXERCISE: Write a summary statement based on your identity in Christ.

CHAPTER VIII
Etiquette

Standard Bearers should be particularly careful when praise dancing with flags. We don't want to be a hinderance or danger to anyone. We also want to be respectful of everyone around us including leaders, members, children, camera operators and other worshipers. Below are a few basic etiquette suggestions.

RESPECT

- Always ask the pastor or worship arts leader for permission to minister with flags, especially when you are a visitor.
- Be prepared to explain what the ministry is about if you are asked.

LOCATION

- Ask the pastor or worship arts leader where they prefer you to minister with flags.

- When choosing an area, be mindful of your location and carefully consider how you might impact the service or worship environment. Are you near a door where people enter and exit? An aisle? On stage? In front of the alter? In the rear? Where are the camera operators? Where are the cords? Will you be blocking anyone's view? Are little children running around? Your goal is to enhance the worship experience, not to be an annoyance, hinderance or hazard.

MODESTY

- Consider your wardrobe choice carefully,
    - Avoid low cut tops that expose cleavage or chest, especially when bending forward.
    - Avoid short tops that expose midriff when arms are lifted.
    - Avoid sheer (see through) clothing.
    - Wear loose fitting garments that allow you to move freely and comfortably.
    - Avoid short or tight dresses, skirts or pants.
    - Avoid excessive makeup and jewelry.

SAFETY

- Be careful not to hit anyone with your flags or other worship tool.
- **Always be aware of your surroundings.** Watch out for people walking or moving around you. If your flags have poles or weights, hitting someone could cause injury. In addition, repeated infractions pose a legitimate safety concern. Standard Bearers should be careful not to hurt the people around them. Our first ministry is love. If the space you are in is too small to minister with flags, consider ministering in a different way (praise, pray for people, intercede, etc.)

CHAPTER IX
Pure Ministry

Pure worship is keeping the main thing the main thing. Jesus Christ is the main thing. It is through Him that we are cleansed and forgiven. It is through Holy Spirit that we are transformed into holy vessels for our Heavenly Father's use. Our Father has given us grace through His son, Jesus Christ, to accomplish His will, which is to have a holy people that live to worship Him; not because we have to, but because we want to.

But the hour cometh, and now is, when the true worshippers shall worship the Father in spirit and in truth: for the Father seeketh such to worship him. John 4:23

In its most authentic expression, pure worship allows people to witness our worship as a Testimony of Christ. In other words, we worship God and allow people to witness the interaction. Our worship speaks where words fail and reminds us how sweet true intimacy is with our Heavenly Father.

Give unto the LORD the glory due unto his name: bring an offering and come before him: **worship the LORD in the beauty of holiness.**
1 Chronicles 16:29

Preparation for God's Use

Many people are drawn to worship arts ministry because they have talents and they want to use them for God. However, if we choose to devote our God-given gifts and talents to God, we need to be aware that our God does not share. Nor does He accept worship offered to idols[102] or anything that is impure. If we desire to use our creative talent to worship a holy God, it must be **sanctified** (pure, legitimate and **set apart**) for His use. We must be willing to submit our self to the process of being **consecrated** (ordained, dedicated to God, sacred) and **purified** (cleansed, decontaminated, purged, delivered). **Refinement** (removal of impurities; honing, polishing) happens as we grow in the Word of God and in pursuit of **holiness**. Refinement is the process of testing. It is compared to the treatment of gold.[103] This preparation process requires dying daily to self. He must increase, so we must decrease.[104] This process is necessary to rid yourself of the old nature and allow God's new nature to take control of your soul.

For example, if your talent is singing, and you've been singing secular songs in nightclubs for a long time, the Lord may require you to stop singing for a while so He can spend time with you;

---

[102] 1 Corinthians 10:7, 14, 1 John 5:21, Colossians 3:5, Jonah 2:8, Galatians 4:8
[103] Isaiah 48:10, 1 Peter 1:6-7, Proverbs 17:3, Malachi 3:24, Zacharia 13:9
[104] John 3:30

purifying and perfecting **you and your gift** for his use. If you are unwilling to surrender to this process, you risk bringing the world into your worship, which corrupts your ministry.

Talents and Gifts are not the Anointing

Everything that looks good is not anointed. Many people in the body of Christ mistake talent and gifts for the anointing. Everything pretty, clever, talented and creative, even with scripture or religious raiment thrown on it, is not anointed. What is the anointing? It is God's empowerment for service; His power to prepare us to serve Him and the people of the world, including those who don't know Him as the true and living God. The anointing is accompanied by signs, wonders, miracles and the power of God. The anointing breaks the yoke of bondage, which is sin. It brings sinners to repentance. It leads the lost to salvation. People have become so enthralled with being entertained with gifts and talent that they are easily deceived. In Christian circles, the word *anointed* has become as casual as the word *love*. Mature Christians should be able to discern gifting from anointing. Until they do, scores of Christians will continue to be deceived and destroyed.[105]

Will You Surrender Your Gifts to God?

When we answer the Lord's call, it means leaving the world behind. It means dedicating our gifts and talents to Him for His exclusive use. He is a jealous God. He does not share.[106] He has called us out

---

[105] Job 36:12, Proverbs 5:23, Proverbs 10:21, Hosea 4:6
[106] Exodus 3:14

of the world and instructs us not to give what is holy to dogs or to cast our pearls before swine.[107] We are to treasure our relationship with God and understand the importance of protecting that which is sacred because if we give our most precious treasure away to people, they will abuse it. Sadly, when talented people seek accolades and acknowledgement from men, they discover that man only cares about man. When we devote our gifts to God, we can be sure that God's reward is better than man's prize.[108] Truly, we will never find complete fulfillment using our gifts and talents for anyone except the one that gave them to us in the first place. Worldly success does not equal inner joy, nor does it lead to eternal rewards. When we offer our God-given gifts and talents back to God, He shares His own spirit and anoints our gift with power for the work of the ministry and for His glory. Without God, it's just a show – mere entertainment; and although that may satisfy the average spectator, it will not break strongholds, heal the sick or draw a sinner to repentance. That is the true purpose for our gifts, but to operate in that level of power requires sacrifice.

There should be nothing we are not willing to give up for God.

I'm afraid we have lost our fear of God. In worship and other things, people tend to think that God should be satisfied with whatever they choose to offer Him. They say, "God knows my heart and it's nobody's business how I worship Him. It's personal." They are

---

[107] Matthew 7:6
[108] Proverbs 18:16

correct about one thing; God does know our heart and that is where the problem lies. We cannot fool or manipulate God, no matter how hard we try. Even when we are self-deceived, God is not deceived. He knows our true motivation for everything we do. He knows that deep down in our soul there is hard-hearted rebellion that is saying, "I'm going to do what I want to do." Yes, God knows our heart very well; better than we will ever know it.

In this chapter, we will examine examples of offerings and worship that God rejected in the Bible to understand why he rejected them. If we are honest, we will see ourselves in these examples. If we cannot see our own sin, our deception is not rooted in ignorance, but rather pride. Pride is the devil's anointing. As we examine the following lessons in the Word of God, please use this time and resource as an opportunity to confront your sin, confess and repent from everything that is not pleasing to God. We cannot defend sin to God. Pure worship can only be made from a pure heart and that is the only kind of worship God is interested in.

Strange Fire

*And Nadab and Abihu, the sons of Aaron, took either of them his censer, and put fire therein, and put incense thereon, and **offered strange fire before the LORD, which he commanded them not**. And there went out fire from* *the LORD, and devoured them, and **they died** before the LORD. Then Moses said unto Aaron, "This is it that the LORD spake, saying**, I will be sanctified in them that come nigh me**, and before all the people I will be glorified." And Aaron held his peace.* Leviticus 10:1-3

When the burnt offering was done according to God's instructions, He would consume the offering to show his acceptance.[109] Nadab and Abihu had been trained **exactly** how to make the offering,[110] but **they decided to do it their way**. Their strange Fire was **unauthorized**. The consequence was death. Thank God the death penalty that we deserve was paid by our Savior. Jesus Christ is our advocate who makes constant intercession for us.[111] Nevertheless, God's character does not change. He is the same yesterday, today and forever, and He has made it clear that He will not accept just any kind of offering or worship. He commands obedience over sacrifices.[112]

Cain & Abel

In Genesis 4, Cain and Abel, the firstborn sons of Adam and Eve, both made offerings to God. Abel's offering (the **first** of his flock **and** the fat) was accepted by God and Cain's offering (fruit from the

---

[109] Leviticus 9:24,
[110] Leviticus 8-9
[111] 1 John 2:1-2
[112] 1 Samuel 15:22, Psalm 51:17

ground) was not. Cain made the mistake of offering God what he wanted to give him instead of what God commanded of him. When his offering was rejected, instead of humbling himself to God, he became jealous and angry. Cain spoke to his brother, but instead of inquiring about how he could please God, he allowed his anger to grow and fester until, in a murderous rage, Cain killed his brother, Abel. God gave Cain a choice; to do well and be accepted or to do wrong and give in to sin.[113] He chose the latter and paid the consequences. God's rejection exposed what was in Cain's heart. His heart was evil; therefore, his works were also evil.[114]

We can learn a few things about ourselves from this story. How often have we chosen wrong over right? Evil over good? Envy over being happy for someone? We are all guilty, but when we submit to God, Holy Spirit transforms our heart and our responses will change as we accept our identity in Christ and take responsibility for our actions.

1. What is in our heart will be exposed through our words and deeds. So, *Let the words of my mouth, and the meditation of my heart, be acceptable in thy sight, O LORD, my strength, and my redeemer.* Psalm 19:14

2. We always have a choice; to do right and be accepted; or do wrong and open the door to sin in our life. *Let us make the decision for ourselves as to what is right; let us have the knowledge among ourselves of what is good.* Job 34:4

---

[113] Genesis 4
[114] Hebrews 11:4, 1 John 3:12, Jude 1:11

3. Jealousy, anger and envy lead to violence (and even murderous behavior). *And the evil spirit from the LORD was upon Saul, as he sat in his house with his javelin in his hand: and David played with his hand. And Saul sought to smite David even to the wall with the javelin: but he slipped away out of Saul's presence, and he smote the javelin into the wall: and David fled, and escaped that night.* 1 Samuel 19: 9-10

4. Gossip, backbiting and slander are sins and a type of murder called *character assassination*. Christians that engage in this behavior should know that it nullifies their testimony as followers of Christ. *If any man among you seem to be religious, and bridleth not his tongue, but deceiveth his own heart, this man's religion is vain.* James 1:26

5. We need to train ourselves to speak kind words, even to our enemies, as the Lord commands. *But I say unto you, Love your enemies, bless them that curse you, do good to them that hate you, and pray for them which despitefully use you, and persecute you...* Matthew 5:44

6. We should refrain from envy, which is coveting or desiring something someone else has. What you see is not the whole picture. Plus, you may not be willing to pay the price to have what someone else has. Focus on what God has for you. Jesus asked His disciples, *Are ye able to drink of the cup that I*

> *shall drink of, and to be baptized with the baptism that I am baptized with?* [115] Of course, they said, *Yes!*. We are still saying *Yes!* today, but we want to skip the crucifixion. We forget that we must die with Christ to reign with Him.[116]

We are encouraged by Apostle Paul who reminds us; *I am crucified with Christ: nevertheless I live; yet not I, but Christ liveth in me: and the life which I now live in the flesh I live by the faith of the Son of God, who loved me, and gave himself for me.* Galatians 2:20

We should desire good things for others. The way we respond when someone is promoted or receives favor from God reveals our heart.[117] It's remarkable how God extends favor to people that are genuinely happy for others. If we have not yet received what we have asked for, we should check our heart for jealousy, envy and covetousness and repent, if necessary. Then, continue to trust God knowing our time will come in due season. If we are faithful in the little things, God will give us more responsibility. So, celebrate with others to prepare your heart to receive your blessing.

Saying, "The Lord knows my heart" and offering Him whatever we choose to give Him, instead of what He commands is an indication of a rebellious heart toward God.

---

[115] Matthew 20:22-28
[116] 2 Timothy 2:11-12
[117] 1 Samuel 19:24

Ananias and Sapphira

Ananias, whose name means *whom Jehovah has graciously given* and Sapphira, whose name means *beautiful or sapphire,* were a married couple that witnessed genuine love and affection among believers. They saw people selling property and land and giving it to the Apostles for distribution, so that everyone was provided for. They wanted **to be known** for the same kind of love, but their motives were insincere. They sold their property, **like they had seen others do**, but held back some of the proceeds. When asked if the amount they gave was the total payment they received for the land they both lied, saying it was the entire amount they received. Their sin was lying to the Holy Spirit and the penalty was death. The husband lied, died and was carried away first; then his wife, who arrived later, did the exact same thing. As a result, fear came upon the church, but the people did not run away. They drew near to the Lord through the preaching of the Gospel. The church grew in the fear of the Lord; proving that the fear (reverence, awe, respect, love) of the Lord does not repel people seeking salvation, but rather draws them to holiness.

And unto man he said, Behold, ***the fear of the LORD****, that **is wisdom;** and **to depart from evil is understanding.*** Job 28:28

How far will you go to be recognized by others? Would you fake speaking in tongues to be accepted by men? Would you lie about your giving? Would you bow your head and pretend to pray when you are really thinking about other things? We lie to the Holy Spirit all the time, but there are consequences for unrepented sin. We may not drop dead today, but we step away from the presence of a holy God with each willful, unrepented sin. However, there is good news. God is merciful and forgiving and with each step we take back, he is still only a confession away. We need only acknowledge our sin to God in genuine repentance to receive forgiveness and grace that covers our sin as we are transformed by His love, His Word and His power.

If we confess our sins, he is faithful and just to forgive us our sins, and to cleanse us from all unrighteousness. If we say that we have not sinned, we make him a liar, and his word is not in us. 1 John 1:9-10

The Danger of Comparison & Competition

*For there shall arise false Christs, and false prophets**, and shall shew great signs and wonders**; insomuch that, if it were possible**, they shall deceive the very elect**.* Matthew 24:24

Even mature Christians will be fooled by signs and wonders performed by people that are not authorized by God. Some, being under a strong delusion, may even be deceived by their own works.[118]

---

[118] Matthew 7:21-23

Therefore, do not be a follower. Do not desire the gifts in someone else. Do not compare yourself with what is popular. Learn what God desires from you and be faithful in whatever it is, even if it is not what you consider glamorous. If you are faithful and obedient, your gifts will make room for you and bring you before great men[119] as evidenced by the lives of Esther, Ruth, Joseph, David, and more. Many who have come from humble beginnings are used by God because He KNOWS them. He has a personal relationship with them. Therefore, do not concern yourself with how successful someone else appears to be. Things may not be as they appear. The Bible tells us not to believe every spirt, but to test the spirits to know if they are of God.[120] Ask God for discernment (the ability to judge well).

Seek intimacy with God above all else.

Idolatry

I will not spend time talking about our fetish for clothing, shoes, makeup, hair and other material things; or our addiction to sports and food; or even the pride that lifts itself high in our heart concerning our gifts, talents and accomplishments, which are all forms of idolatry; but I will share what the Lord specifically commanded me to share.

---

[119] Proverbs 18:16
[120] 1 John 4:1-3

Following are three examples of what God calls idolatry in the Holy Bible. These abominations have found a place in the heart and soul of Christians (His church) and the Lord wants them rooted out.

Wherefore come out from among them, and be ye separate, saith the Lord, and touch not the unclean thing; and I will receive you. [121]
2 Corinthians 6:17

Wisdom and Intellect Cannot Rationalize Idolatry

Take a lesson from the wisest man of all, King Solomon. The appeasement of hundreds of foreign wives and their false gods led to his downfall. He was warned (twice), but like many of us, he chose to do what he wanted to do instead of what God commanded.[122] Solomon, in all his wisdom, allowed his lust to corrupt his soul and the souls of those that followed him. Sadly, there is no evidence that Solomon ever repented. In fact, the shrines of the temples that Solomon built were still standing when Josiah became king.[123] In contrast, *King Josiah, being utterly convicted by the Law of the Lord, destroyed all the shrines, alters and graven images of the false gods in high places,* [124]*as did King Hezekiah before him.* Some people study higher education and become Bible scholars and theologians but neglect to surrender their intellect to God. If in all their getting, they do not get understanding and they practice

---

[121] 1 John 5:21
[122] 1 King 3:3-4, 11:4-13, 2 Kings 23:13, Nehemiah 13:26
[123] 2 Kings 23:4-20
[124] 2 Kings 18:1-6

idolatry (even calling God's laws legalism or religion to avoid obeying God), no amount of education or knowledge can save them. The Word of God still declares them fools.

Professing themselves to be wise, they became fools… [125] Romans 1:22

Yoga

*"And what agreement hath the temple of God with idols? for ye are the temple of the living God; as God hath said, I will **dwell in them**, and **walk in them**; and I will be their God, and they shall be my people.* 2 Corinthians 6:16

If our God hates carved images that are made of nothing but wood, stone and minerals, how much more does he hate it when we use our bodies (His Holy Temple) to bow down to false gods – even in ignorance for which there is really no excuse because the truth is not hidden.

Statue of Shiva "The Destroyer" performing yogic meditation in lotus

As for Christian Yoga; Christianity and Hinduism do not mix. You are either one or the other. You cannot be both. The God of Christianity does not share His authority, His throne or His people with other gods. The true and living God created our bodies to

---

[125] Romans Chapter 1 (entire chapter)

worship Him alone. He does not ask us to empty our mind. He calls us to meditate on His Word day and night.[126] Our God does not instruct us to empty our mind. He keeps us in perfect peace when our mind is fixed on Him.[127] We don't want to be yoked (in union) with anything but His Holy Spirit. In addition, the churches acceptance of this idolatrous practice poses a stumbling block to new Christians; some of whom simply integrate Christian customs and traditions into their New Age or foreign theology…and they end up in worse condition (spiritually) than before they were introduced to a compromising church.

Facts about Yoga[128]

1. Yoga was first introduced in the U.S.A. in the late **19th Century.**
2. The most popular type of Yoga in the U.S.A. is **Hatha Yoga.**
3. Yoga originated in **India.**
4. Yoga is inspired by practices in **Hinduism, Buddhism and Jainism.**
5. The word yoga means yoke or **union.**
6. **Shiva is** regarded as the patron god of yoga, meditation and arts.
7. Shiva is known as the *creator, maintainer* and *the destroyer*.

---

[126] Joshua 1:8
[127] Isaiah 26:3
[128] Wikipedia.org

8. In Shaivism tradition, Shiva is the Supreme being who creates, protects and transforms the universe.
9. In yoga, each pose is dedicated to a specific false god, and there are over 330 million gods.

Spiritually Speaking

As yoga poses are performed, the spirit of Shiva (the Destroyer) and every false god and demon attached to this practice are invited into the soul of a Christian worshiper. Based on this revelation, struggles with anger, jealousy, manipulation, lying, sexual sins and the like may be a direct result of the spirits that have been invited into the secret place that is reserved for the true and living God. Because there are so many false gods (idols) intertwined in yoga, the devil can deceive Christians that practice yoga with strong delusions. *Yoga isn't bad. It's just exercise. You're not worshiping false God's. How dare this Christian tell you that yoga is bad. They are just being legalistic....Now, let's do COBRA!*

Many people that practice yoga will strongly defend it against the knowledge of the One True God.

So, how do we purge ourselves of these parasitical spirits?
By repenting (turning away from this idolatrous practice), renouncing Shiva, the god of yoga and all other false gods associated with this religious practice. We should also educate Christian leaders about the sin of idolatry associated with the practice of yoga in the Christian church.

Furthermore, we must also purge ourselves of these evil spirits by relying on the spiritual weapons provided in the Word of God to repel these spiritual foes.

*(For the weapons of our warfare **are not carnal**, **but mighty through God** to the pulling down of strong holds;) **Casting down imaginations**, and **every high thing that exalteth itself against the knowledge of God**, and **bringing into captivity every thought to the obedience of Christ**.*. 2 Corinthians 10:4-5

*Finally, my brethren, **be strong in the Lord**, and in the **power of his might**. Put on the whole armour of God, that ye may be able to stand against the wiles of the devil. For **we wrestle not against flesh and blood,** but against principalities, against powers, against the rulers of the darkness of this world, against spiritual wickedness in high places. Wherefore take unto you the whole armour of God, that ye may be able to withstand in the evil day, and having done all, to stand. Stand therefore, **having your loins girt about with** truth [Jesus is the way, the truth and the light], and having on the **breastplate of righteousness** [our righteousness is in Him]; And your **feet shod** with the preparation of the gospel of peace [to face evil with no fear, but the peace that the gospel gives us]. Above all, taking **the shield of faith** [our protection from evil], wherewith ye shall be able to quench all the fiery darts of the wicked. And take the **helmet of salvation** [we have the mind of Christ], and the **sword of the Spirit, which is the word of God**.*. Ephesians 6:10-17

However, be warned, these spirits will not go quietly. They have become quite comfortable in their home. The Bible tells us that when a house is swept clean, the unclean spirit walks through dry places and when it finds no rest, it returns to the house it came from, and when it finds it clean, it goes out and finds seven more spirits, more wicked than itself, and they come back and take possession of the home, and the state of the person is worse than before.[129] Jesus said this was the fate of our wicked generation. Therefore, when you repent and receive forgiveness, do not go back to that unclean thing. There are spiritually healthy alternatives to yoga. (e.g. stretching, toning and PraiseMoves)[130].

And be not conformed to this world: but be ye transformed by the renewing of your mind, that ye may prove what is that good, and acceptable, and perfect, will of God. Romans 12:2

For ye are bought with a price: therefore glorify God in your body, and in your spirit, which are God's. 1 Corinthians 6:20

If we arrogantly attempt to love the world, entertain evil spirits and command the authority of Christ, all at the same time, we are living under a strong delusion of deception. Even if we do good works, perform signs and wonders in the name of God and have the adoration of men, it may very well be the spiritual influence of 330 million false gods working iniquity within us to deceive the people

---

[129] Matthew 12:43-45
[130] Praisemoves.com is the Christian ALTERNATIVE to yoga.

of God that ignorantly follow us and call everything we do anointed. We are responsible for leading those that follow us into deception.

Iniquity means "in violation of law" via ignorance or contempt (disrespect, scorn, disdain).

Many will say to me in that day, Lord, Lord, have we not prophesied in thy name? and in thy name have cast out devils? and in thy name done many wonderful works? And then will I profess unto them, I never knew you: depart from me, ye that work iniquity. Matthew 7:22-23

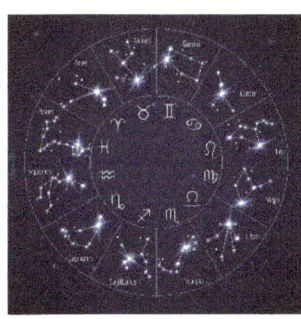

Astrology

In the Book of Genesis, God created the world. He clearly stated the purpose of the things He created. In Chapter 1 verses 14 and 15, God tells us the purpose for the stars.

*And God said, Let there be lights in the firmament of the heaven **to divide the day from the night; and let them be for signs**, and **for seasons, and for days, and years**: And let them be for lights in the firmament of the heaven to give light upon the earth: and it was so.*

1) To divide day from night;
2) to be signs;
3) to distinguish seasons;
4) to separate days and years.

In Genesis 1:16-18, The Word of God tells us the purpose for the sun and moon.

And God made two great lights; the greater light to rule the day, and the lesser light to rule the night: he made the stars also. And God set them in the firmament of the heaven **to give light upon the earth,** *And* **to rule over the day and over the night, and to divide the light from the darkness**: *and God saw that it was good.*

The sun, moon and stars also have a specific purpose ordained by God.

1) To give light upon the earth;
2) To rule over the day and over the night
3) To divide the light from the darkness

Neither the sun, moon or stars were created to be objects of worship.

We should heed the prophecy given to the Jewish people concerning people that practiced astrology:

And they [the bones of the people of Jerusalem] shall spread them before the sun, and the moon, and all the host of heaven, whom they have loved, and whom they have served, and after whom they have walked, and whom they have sought, and whom they have worshipped: they shall not be gathered, nor be buried; they shall be for dung upon the face of the earth. Jeremiah 8:2

King Josiah did away with the pagan priests appointed by the kings of Judah to burn incense on the high places of the towns of Judah and on those around Jerusalem – **those who burned incense to**

Baal, to the sun and moon, to the constellations and to all the starry hosts.[131]

Astrology is not harmless

Now, you may say, I don't worship the sun, moon and stars, but if you associate yourself with an astrology sign and allow it to define your personality and direct your future, it is a form of worship and an offense to God because that is not what he created them for. He made man and woman in His own image and likeness.[132] Therefore, when you give credit to His creation for what He created, it is idolatry – worship of another God. Jehovah God wants your identity and your destiny to be rooted in Him and Him alone. God was so serious about this issue that in the Old Testament, He instituted the death penalty for violation of this law. But, even in this harsh punishment, God required proof. Therefore, the people were **accountable to one another**, as well as to God.

God never intended for us to use the constellations to tell our fortune, direct our future or describe our personality.

There are consequences for disobedience

Although we are not stoned today for practicing astrology, when we are corrected or warned about it, we should allow the Word of God to minister to our heart, so we can be free. In the body of Christ, we are accountable to one another.

---

[131] 2 King 23:5
[132] Genesis 1:27

If you practice astrology, tarot cards, play with the Ouija board, believe fortune cookies or practice any magic arts, repent in pursuit of God. Do not be deceived. These are diviners' tools and variants of witchcraft. Repent and allow God to confirm your identity in Him through His Word. Put your faith in Him exclusively and you will be blessed.

When we look to the sun, moon and stars for direction and consultation, it displeases God.

If Astrology is a stronghold in your life, pray and meditate on the following scriptures.

If there be found among you, within any of thy gates which the LORD thy God giveth thee, man or woman, that hath wrought wickedness in the sight of the LORD thy God, in transgressing his covenant, And hath gone and served other gods, and worshipped them, either the sun, or moon, or any of the host of heaven, which I have not commanded; And it be told thee, and thou hast heard of it, and enquired diligently, and, behold, it be true, and the thing certain, that such abomination is wrought in Israel: Then shalt thou bring forth that man or that woman, which have committed that wicked thing, unto thy gates, even that man or that woman, and shalt stone them with stones, till they die. Deuteronomy 17:2-5

The houses in Jerusalem and those of the kings of Judah will be defiled like this place, Topheth–all the houses where they burned incense on the roofs to all the starry hosts and poured out drink offerings to other gods. Jeremiah 19:13

Those who bow down on the roofs to worship the starry host, those who bow down and swear by the LORD and who also swear by Molech, those who turn back from following the LORD and neither seek the LORD nor inquire of him. Be silent before the Sovereign LORD, for the day of the LORD is near. The LORD has prepared a sacrifice; he has consecrated those he has invited. On the day of the Lord's sacrifice I will punish the princes and the king's sons and all those clad in foreign clothes. Zephaniah 1:5-8

You have lifted up the shrine of your king, the pedestal of your idols, the star of your god — which you made for yourselves. "Therefore, I will send you into exile beyond Damascus," says the LORD, whose name is God Almighty. Amos 5:26-27

Isis Wings

As mentioned in the Chapter entitled *Flag Styles and Worship Tools*, Isis Wings have received a makeover in an attempt to make them acceptable for Christian worship. Christian bookstores renamed and repackaged them as *Angel Wings* and worship dancers now use them in Christian ministry. Isis wings are used by belly dancers and personify the goddess, Isis.
Currently, this garment is being used by

Isis Wings were renamed Angel Wings, sold in Christian bookstores and are now used in worship arts ministry in the church.

liturgical dancers to worship the true and living God. In my research, I even found a web site where a Christian minister made wings exactly like Isis wings, and proceeded to explain why they were an acceptable form of Christian worship. So, if we look hard enough for someone to agree with us on this topic or any topic, there are people out there that will back us up. However, we must learn to rely on the Word of God and Holy Spirit, who *speaks what He hears the Father speak.*[133]

These wings come in a variety of colors and are quite spectacular. The most popular color seems to be gold lame. Gold is the color that represents God's glory. Do you believe that our God accepts a replica of a false god as worship? If so, you are sadly mistaken. It is an abomination to Him.

Statue of the goddess, Isis

Who is Isis?

According to mythology, Isis was a major **goddess** in ancient Egyptian **religion**. She was the first daughter of Geb, **god of the Earth**, and Nut, **goddess of the Sky**. Isis married her brother, Osiris. They had a son together and named him Horus. According to mythology, Isis resurrected Osiris when he was murdered by Set by using incantations (magic spells). Her **magic power** was said to be more powerful than all other gods. She was believed to **help the dead into the afterlife** as she had done for

---

[133] John 16:13

Osiris. The name, Isis, means ***throne***. Isis is called the goddess of health, marriage and wisdom.[134]

> *What we wear when we come into the presence of the King to worship Him matters, especially if it resembles an idol.*

*And thou shalt put upon Aaron the **holy garments**, and **anoint him**, and **sanctify him**; that he may minister unto me **in the priest's office**.* Exodus 40:13

We are priests and Kings.[135] Consider how important the garments worn by the priests were in the original tabernacle.[136] God designed them himself. Isis Wings represent a false god and is not something Kingdom Standard Bearers or praise dancers should wear in the presence of our holy King. Please do not confuse this issue with legalism and religion. This is not about clothes; although there is a strong case for modesty in the church these days.[137] This is about idolatry – the worship of other gods. We should abstain from even the appearance of evil when pursuing pure ministry.[138]

> *To be clear, Isis Wings is not appropriate attire for Worship Arts Ministry or the Ministry of the Standard Bearer because it is founded in iniquity.*

---

[134] SOURCE: Wikipedia.org

[135] Revelation 1:6, 5:10; 1 Peter 2:9-10, 1 Peter 2:5, Isaiah 62:3

[136] Exodus 28:2, 40; 35, 39; Leviticus 8, 16

[137] 1 Timothy 2:8-10, 1 Peter 3:1-4, Proverbs 11:22

[138] 1 Thessalonians 5:22

How should we respond to correction about something we thought was okay, but we are being told it is wrong in the eyes of God?

Hear counsel, and receive instruction, that thou mayest be wise in thy latter end. There are many devices in a man's heart; nevertheless, the counsel of the LORD, that shall stand. Proverbs 19:20-21

1. Do not become defensive; even if the information is not delivered tactfully.
2. Thank the messenger for giving you something to consider.
3. Ask God to reveal His heart to you concerning the matter.
4. Be willing to surrender tradition, religion and past beliefs about the matter.
5. Verify the information by praying and researching (using the Bible, commentaries, a concordance and/or historical books). The most important thing is to allow Holy Spirit to lead and guide you into all truth, rather than focusing on proving your point of view or belief.
6. If you discover the information to be true, repent. (Ask God for forgiveness and turn away from the tradition, habit or sin.)
7. Replace it with something that truly glorifies God or abandon it altogether.

But seek ye first the kingdom of God, and his righteousness; and all these things shall be added unto you. Matthew 6:33

Repentance in Action

One of my favorite stories of repentance in the Bible is found in the Book of Acts, Chapter 19. When the Jews and Greeks that lived in Ephesus heard about what happened to the sons of Sceva, who attempted to cast out demons in the name and authority of Jesus Christ, and were overrun and beat up by those demons, **fear fell upon them** and the name of the Lord was magnified. Many that believed came and **confessed** and **showed their deeds**. They went as far as to **burn their books of curious arts**, and the Bible tells us the value of the books was great,[139] but they did not care. When God's truth is revealed to our heart, our love for Him should overrule any perceived benefit of holding onto anything in this world.

---

[139] Acts 19:19

CHAPTER X
In Conclusion

For as we have many members in one body, and all members have not the same office: So we, being many, are one body in Christ, and every one members one of another. Having then gifts differing according to the grace that is given to us, whether prophecy, let us prophesy according to the proportion of faith; Or ministry, let us wait on our ministering: or he that teacheth, on teaching; Or he that exhorteth, on exhortation: he that giveth, let him do it with simplicity; he that ruleth, with diligence; he that sheweth mercy, with cheerfulness. Romans 12:4-8

It's a wonderful thing to discover where you fit in the body of Christ - what your unique gift is to the body. It is great to know how to operate in your gift and to use it to glorify God and edify the body of Christ, but God can do even more with you through your obedience. Some people get so caught up in their gift that it becomes an idol in their life. They end up chasing the gift, stocking up on tools and adornments and looking for any opportunity to use their new stuff and demonstrate their talent. They don't listen to God because they already know what they want to do, so they move full speed ahead. Just because you have discovered your gift, doesn't mean that you are doing what God wants you to do with it, unless you are seeking Him for direction.

In all thy ways acknowledge him, and he shall direct thy paths.
Proverbs 3:6

Some people think they need to chase opportunities, but if you are willing to completely surrender your gifts to God, He is *able to do exceeding, abundantly above all that we ask or think, according to the power that works in us.* [140] The most important thing to know about gifts is they belong to God and are given to be used for His purpose. How can you know the best use of your gift and the best time to use it unless you seek the one who gave it to you? Therefore, don't worship the gift. Worship the gift giver.

---
*May God bless you as He cleanses and purifies
you for greater works in His name.*
---

[140] Ephesians 3:20

List of Illustrations

Page   Description

3   Arletia and step-daughter, Shekinah Mayfield 2017 (personal photo)

4   Banner at Southside Christian Fellowship in Georgia (personal photo)

7   Praying hands on Bible (BigStock photo)

10   Xavier Mayfield at Southside Christian Fellowship in Georgia 2018 (personal photo)

27   Civil War Soldiers (BigStock photo)

30   International Prayer Warriors of Papua New Guinea 2018 (personal photo)

35   Aaron and Hur holding up Moses' hands (public domain 1873)

44   Banners (Used with permission of Rhonda Holbrook)

45   Standard Bearers (from The Journey 2016 stage production by Solid Rock Church in Monroe, Ohio)

49   Standard Bearers (from The Journey 2016 stage production by Solid Rock Church in Monroe, Ohio)

55   Standards of the Twelve Tribes of Israel (graphic design by Franklin Mayfield)

56   Breastplate of High Priest (Creative Commons: Attribution: Dr. Avishai Teicher Pikiwiki Israel. PikiWiki Israel 34561 Breastplate on the front of the central Sephardic.JPG)

57-71   Standards of the Twelve Tribes of Israel (graphic design by Franklin Mayfield)

80   Banners (Used with permission of Rhonda Holbrook)

80   Worship Flags (Used with permission of Rhonda Holbrook)

81   Swing Flags (Used by permission of Meghan Williams, Dyed4You.com)

81   Large Pole Flags (from The Journey 2016 stage production by Solid Rock Church in Monroe, Ohio)

81   Billows (from The Journey 2016 stage production by Solid Rock Church in Monroe, Ohio)
82   Large Hanging Banner at Southside Christian Fellowship in Georgia (personal photo)
82   Scarf (BigStock photos)
83   Worship Streamer (Used by permission of Meghan Williams, Dyed4You.com)
83   Tabrets (Design and photo by Arletia Mayfield)
84   Worship Garments (Arletia Mayfield personal photo)
84   Isis Wings (BigStock photos)
87   For the Love of God Book Cover (photo: Summer Allen Typography: Franklin Mayfield)
88   Arletia Mayfield Personal photo
99   The sin of Nadab and Abihu (public domain from 1907 Bible card)
100   Speculum Humanae Salvationis Production: Germany; 15th century. (unknown artist. Public domain. SOURCE: British Museum)
104   The death of Ananias by Raphael (public domain 1515 wikipedia)
108   Statue of Shiva, the Destroyer, performing yogic meditation in lotus position (licensed under Creative Commons: alyan Kumar - originally posted to Flickr as ShivMandir , Kemp Fort)
113   Astrology Wheel (BigStock photos)
117   Isis Wings (BigStock photos)
118   Isis Statue (BigStock photos)
128   Arletia and Franklin Mayfield (personal photo)

BigStock images licensed and used under Standard Content Usage Agreement

The Prophetic Scribe Publications Mandate

The Prophetic Scribe Publications is a Kingdom of God enterprise operating under the direction and guidance of Holy Spirit. We publish Christian media with a Kingdom focus that ministers to all people to help them receive forgiveness and salvation through Jesus Christ, deliverance from the bondage of sin and to grow in maturity through the Word of God.

VISION: To promote spiritual growth through media (print, video, audio and theater).

MISSION: To develop strong witnesses for Christ who are not ashamed to proclaim the Testimony of Christ.

PURPOSE: To tear down old legacies and traditions that stand between God and his people so they can experience freedom from condemnation and wholeness through holiness.

"And they overcame him by the blood of the Lamb, and by the word of their testimony; and they loved not their lives unto the death."
~ Revelation 12:11 ~

About Us

Franklin and Arletia Mayfield are ordained ministers, chaplains and missionaries. They travel the U.S.A. and abroad as Media Missionaries. Franklin is the founder of a global Christian Internet Television Network and uses media technology to serve Christian missions, churches and ministries.

Together, they are covenant partners in marriage, ministry and business.

Purchase books and other media by Arletia and Franklin Mayfield: TPS Publications: https://tpspublications.com

Follow our missionary journey:
Mayfield Missions: https://mayfieldmissions.media

For information about our internet media services: trueGOD.tv Corporate: https://info.truegod.tv

To view Christian programs:
trueGOD.tv: https://truegod.tv

www.ingramcontent.com/pod-product-compliance
Lightning Source LLC
Chambersburg PA
CBHW040108100526
44584CB00029BA/3927